Focus on Collaborative Learning

Focus on Collaborative Learning

Classroom Practices in Teaching English, 1988

Jeff Golub, Chair,
and the Committee on Classroom Practices

National Council of Teachers of English
1111 Kenyon Road, Urbana, Illinois 61801

NCTE Editorial Board: Donald R. Gallo, Thomas Newkirk, Raymond Rodrigues, Dorothy Strickland; L. Jane Christensen, *ex officio*; John Lansingh Bennett, *ex officio*

Book Design: Tom Kovacs for TGK Design

Staff Editor: Tim Bryant

NCTE Stock Number 17538

Library of Congress Catalog Card Number 85-644740

Contents

Introduction

Every lesson plan, classroom activity, and instructional method reflects certain assumptions about what's worth knowing, how students learn, and what the function of the teacher is. Giving a lecture on the importance and structure of the topic sentence, for instance, implies that this is information worth knowing, that students learn best by absorbing facts and other material, and that the teacher's role is that of dispenser of information. An interest in collaborative learning has grown because of some assumptions that are changing in one or more of these areas of English instruction. Teachers are finding that an instructional approach emphasizing "peer tutoring and similar modes such as peer criticism and classroom group work" (Bruffee 1984, p. 637) is often an effective way to learn the material at hand and to gain valuable insights. In a comprehensive and articulate essay about cooperative learning, Bruffee characterized the method as "a form of indirect teaching in which the teacher sets the problem and organizes students to work it out collaboratively" (p. 637).

Collaborative learning has as its main feature a structure that allows for student talk: students are *supposed* to talk with each other as they work together on various classroom projects and activities, and it is in this talking that much of the learning occurs. James Britton, for instance, has said that "the relationship of talk to writing is central to the writing process":

> Talk is more expressive—the speaker is not obliged to keep himself in the background as he may be in writing; talk relies on an immediate link with listeners, usually a group or a whole class; the rapid exchanges of conversation allow many things to go on at once—exploration, clarification, shared interpretation, insight into differences of opinion, illustration and anecdote, explanation by gesture, expression of doubt; and if something is not clear you can go on until it is. (Britton et al. 1975, p. 29)

Collaborative learning activities, then, allow students to learn by "talking it out," assimilating their ideas and information through interaction with others. It also changes the role or function of the

1

teacher from "information giver" to "guide on the side," one who is available to respond to the students' emerging insights.

But it is not enough simply to decide that collaborative learning is indeed an appropriate and effective method of instruction; one must also train students to develop specific collaborative learning skills to ensure that they can work productively and harmoniously in pairs and in small groups. Consequently, we have devoted the first section of this book to articles that might help with this problem. These articles identify valuable guidelines to follow in developing students' group skills.

The second section provides descriptions of cooperative learning activities dealing with the study of literature. In the third section, the authors show how a cooperative approach may be used to help students compose, revise, and edit their writing. Finally, we offer several unusual cooperative learning activities that defy simple categorization. The authors describe creative collaborative projects that develop students' language and communication skills in a variety of ways.

The idea of allowing students to work cooperatively on a lesson or classroom project is a most worthwhile approach to English instruction. Establishing the conditions for the successful use of this instructional strategy—and providing examples of such activities—is the focus of this volume.

The members of the Classroom Practices committee hope that this volume will prove to be of value to you and your work in the classroom. I thank those members for the considerable time and effort they spent reading and reviewing manuscripts—Pat Phelan, Carlota Cárdenas de Dwyer, Beverly Busching, Jane Hornburger, and Jay Lalley.

> Jeff Golub, Chair
> Committee on Classroom Practices in Teaching English

References

Britton, J. N., T. Burgess, N. Martin, A. McLeod, and H. Rosen. 1975. *The Development of Writing Abilities (11–18)*. London: Macmillan Education Ltd.

Bruffee, K. A. 1984. Collaborative Learning and the "Conversation of Mankind." *College English* 46: 637.

I Developing Collaborative Learning Skills

1 None of Us Is as Smart as All of Us

Dana Herreman
Newark High School
Newark, Ohio

Mention the group process to me and I get positively rabid with excitement. Remark that you're tired of using groups in class because it's an overused technique and I'm likely to become violent. If you're my supervisor and you tell me you'll come back later when I'm teaching, I'll tell you that I'm teaching some of the most valuable lessons my students will ever learn—in groups.

It's not only because I was both a speech and communications major and an English major in college that I'm an enthusiastic cheerleader for the group process; it's also because I have seen groups work in my classroom over and over again. Each time I watch my students struggle through the process, each time I talk about groups to my colleagues, each time I participate in a problem-solving, discussion, or training group, I renew my commitment to both utilizing and teaching the group process. As teachers, we should do more than use groups only as an occasional break from standard operating procedure; we have a responsibility to *teach* the group process. It is more than a mere teaching technique for a slow day: *the group process is the life process.*

We all have the opportunity to become involved in numerous groups in our lifetimes. We begin in an informal neighborhood group of kids deciding who's "it," and we progress through scouting and fraternities or sororities into professional organizations and boards of directors. There is also, of course, involvement in the most immediate and perhaps essential small group—the family. Because our government is not a dictatorship, every decision made in our society that is not a personal decision is made by a group. Questions are discussed, debated, and decided upon by groups of people, not by a tyrant. We believe in and endorse this system day after day. Your salary was determined by a group process called negotiation.

The textbook you use to teach literature was chosen by a selection committee. The number of hours your students spend in school each day was decided on by a group of legislators. So, in teaching our students how to work effectively in a group setting, we are teaching them far more than that day's material; we are teaching them about democracy and about life, and also about how to live more successfully.

The group process must be *taught*, however. Just because individuals can be configured into a circle does not mean that they will automatically become good communicators. In the past ten years we have discovered that just because we have ears, we (or our students) do not necessarily know how to listen well. Listening is a teachable skill, and so is communicating in a group. Students won't learn good group skills without specific, structured instruction and training.

The Group Process and the Writing Process

Although I use groups and teach group communication in a variety of settings, I have more recently focused on the group process as an integral part of the writing process. After going through my own writing project experience, I have sought ways to integrate group communication into all five steps of the writing process, and into the process as a whole. The prewriting phase, for example, offers many excellent possibilities. One frequent application is using a group of four to seven students to generate ideas in a brainstorming session. Another application of prewriting is in discussion—of a story or poem, a television program, something that happened at school, or a student issue or problem. Prewriting groups are also useful as students complete other prewriting activities, such as cataloging, webbing, and listing. Sharing their work with others and listening to new ideas expand the students' idea base and give them more possibilities to begin drafting.

I imagine that writing teachers rarely think of group activities as useful in the drafting phase of the writing process, but it *is* possible. One way I've used drafting successfully in a group setting is through the discussion test. I've most often used this kind of test over a novel that the students have read outside of class. Again, I organize groups of four to seven (the optimum number for a small group). The students discuss an essay-type question together and then draft a response. Everyone in the group is responsible for participating in both the discussion and the formulation of the answer, and consensus (total agreement) must be reached before the group can put anything in writing. Other opportunities for group drafting include a letter to a guest speaker or an administrator and answering the study questions from the book after reading a piece of literature. The key to success in this stage is to require all students to make contributions to the group's final product.

Revision, too, offers rich opportunities for successful group communication. Since it is at this time that students are encouraged to "tinker" a little or a lot with their writing, exchanging drafts or reading them out loud to a group can spark good discussions of alternatives for the writers. Revision groups are often most effective as problem-solving groups. The group is given a specific amount of time to complete a specific task or solve a specific problem. It is ill-advised to put student writers in a group with the nebulous task of revising their papers. A much more achievable goal is to ask group members to focus on a particular aspect of their papers; for instance, beginnings and endings, or adequate paragraph structure. Group members then read and evaluate each paper in terms of that one aspect. The members should be required to find both good elements and elements that still need revision in all of the papers they are considering.

Editing student compositions is all too often what we teachers end up doing rather than training our students to do it themselves. Once again, using groups can be very effective. There are at least two ways to set up group editing. As with revision groups, assigning a specific task in a specific time period works very well. Instructions such as "You have fifteen minutes to read the papers in your group and find the spelling errors they may contain" tell students exactly what you expect of them. These instructions also motivate the students to get started—not to spend part of the class period discussing last Friday's game. Another opinion is to create work groups, groups that come together to work together. These groups have one specific editing task each time they meet. In a single classroom there could be one group focusing on editing for punctuation errors, another correcting grammar and usage, and another editing for capitalization. On editing day, compositions are circulated from group to group and then returned to the author with each group's suggestions.

The publishing phase of the writing process is sometimes a difficult one for teachers simply because the options for publishing are often rather limited. I define *publishing* as anything that happens to a student's writing after the student has completed all previous steps. Under this definition, simply reading the finished written products to each other in a group setting is a form of publishing. If students are made aware of the steps in the writing process, using group brainstorming or problem-solving sessions to discover new or previously unconsidered methods of publishing their work will be a logical conclusion to a writing assignment. It might also provide the teacher with new ideas for publishing student work. "How can we create new audiences for our writing?" or "In what ways can we make our writing more visible to more people?" are questions that actively involve students in their own publishing. Another publishing option used frequently in classrooms is to have student groups construct their own literary magazines or anthologies that feature student work.

The group process, whether in problem-solving, discussion, training, or work groups, can be extremely effective in teaching the individual steps of the writing process. It can also be utilized creatively for one major assignment that encompasses every step of the writing process. The past few years I have used a writing assignment in my American literature classes called "The *People* Magazine Project," which is done completely in the group setting. In this project students are organized into groups of four to seven, with the optimum number being five; their goal is to create a magazine that spans the period 1840–1890 and is modeled after *People*. The assignment has certain guidelines, including the number of literary and historical persons to be included, illustrations, and so on. The groups are responsible for prewriting and planning the entire magazine, drafting the articles and advertisements, making any necessary revisions, doing the final editing, and ultimately publishing the magazine. My function is to act as advisor and occasionally motivator or arbiter to make sure that the work is being accomplished and that no one group member is being overburdened. The students work in groups for five class periods and outside of class as much as they deem necessary. One person is designated as chairperson to guide the group, settle disputes, and communicate with me. Although there is often much protesting that the group will never finish, never get the required number of articles, never find good illustrations, never get the magazine put together, and that the assignment is altogether unreasonable, the finished products have been excellent—thereby proving the power and creativity inherent in groups.

Group Process Skills

The group communication process truly is a wonderful and effective complement to the writing process, but as mentioned earlier, just because students can be put in a circle doesn't mean they can function as accomplished group communicators. Group skills, which in many ways are simply good communication skills, must be taught, and they must be modeled. Students should be taught the different types and functions of groups: discussion, problem solving, work, and training. Then, when they cluster together as a problem-solving or work group, their purpose is much clearer to them.

Students also need to learn to be effective in the various roles that emerge in group communication. Whether or not a leader is assigned, one will tend to appear in every group setting. Every student should know the responsibilities a leader has, not only because he or she might be the leader tomorrow but also to function as a good group member, assisting the leader with the smooth operation of the group. Isolates or clowns can impede progress toward a goal, but if students are taught that these roles are likely to come out in a group, and if they have some strategies to deal with other students taking on these roles, they will be much less frustrated and will be more likely to succeed. A good activity for teaching roles is to assign each student a role in a particular group which the student does not reveal. After the group interaction, ask students to analyze the effectiveness of the communication, identify which roles were played, and discuss how those roles helped or hindered the group. If the students are able to devise strategies to deal with talkative or non-task-oriented group members, they will be more able to deal with these types every time they are in a group.

Students also need to practice good group behaviors, such as listening, responding, agreeing, disagreeing, clarifying, and making procedural statements. I teach these skills to students in two ways. I sit down with the group and model good listening or good clarifying statements and then encourage them to practice those skills. Or I interrupt. My voice, fortunately, is louder than five or six groups combined, if I want it to be, so I just raise it to the necessary level and tell students to stop for a moment and allow the person to the right of the leader or the one across from the leader to summarize what has been said so far and to make a statement of what the group should do next. A different interruption might require students to stop discussing and individually write down what they think they just heard said in the group. When comparing perceptions, group members will be able to determine whether they were actively listening and participating or just daydreaming. I find a combination of modeling good behavior and interrupting group procedures to be the best way to help students to learn and to begin to incorporate those new skills into the group process.

Evaluation

Evaluating work done in groups can be tricky. It is difficult to penalize all group members because one person didn't do his or her share of the work and consequently the final product is less than expected or required. In using group communication with the writing process, I grade simply on a pass/fail basis (which is how I grade all writing) and give credit for good participation. If the writing has been a major assignment, I might give credit for the writing and also give a group-participation grade to each student. An important aspect of evaluation is having the students evaluate their own work after the group interaction is over. When a group has worked together on a project that takes one class period or more, I have students evaluate the quality of their own participation and that of others in the group. In exchange for confidentiality, students can be very honest about their work and their classmates' work. If the project is to receive a letter grade, I ask students to estimate what grade they themselves should receive, as well as what grade the group should receive. Their estimations are either very close to my own evaluation or the students are harder on themselves than I would be. The student evaluations are very helpful to me if any single person's grade needs to be adjusted upward from the group's grade or (infrequently) downward. Do some kids take advantage of the harder workers and essentially ride their coattails to a better grade than they might deserve? Probably. But we, as teachers, need to be philosophical about this and realize that such people exist in groups in the adult world, too, and that the experience of learning the group process is still valuable enough to keep teaching it. Those overachievers who worked so hard on the group project will continue to be hard workers in their professional organizations or on their boards in the future. By learning the realities of group dynamics as youngsters, they will be better equipped to handle such hangers-on and will face fewer frustrations as adults.

If you have ever sat through a local board of education meeting or a meeting of the executive board of almost any organization, you are probably painfully aware of the fact that good group communication skills are often lacking in "the real world." Simply getting older doesn't endow any of us with effective communication skills. Teaching group communication to our students now will truly help them function in a democratic society in the future. The group process, whether applied to writing, to the teaching of literature, or as an important skill in itself, expands our personal knowledge and our own limited experiences. That fact alone should transform the skeptic to the kind of cheerleader I am for the group process. After all, it really is true that none of us is as smart as all of us.

2 Collaborative Learning and Other Disasters

Richard Whitworth
Ball State University

I was brought up in a traditional school setting, in which the roles of the teacher and students were clearly defined. The teacher bawled into our ears for fifty minutes, perhaps on the fox-hunting outfits in *Silas Marner,* and we took notes. Or the teacher demanded a 485-word essay—no fewer words—on "roadside beauty," and we students obliged.

Later, when I began to teach, I did exactly the same thing. It was "teach as I was taught": the lessons were ground out, the desks were evenly spaced, a feet-on-the-floor atmosphere was maintained at all times.

During those early years of teaching, I was disturbed by the glazed eyes of my seventh graders, the bored and disdainful curve of their mouths, and their fidgeting, overactive feet. I knew something was wrong, but I decided the fault must be with these inner-city kids, not with me or my lessons.

About this time, I came upon the gospel of James Moffett (1968b). I was appalled. The man advocated a student-centered language arts curriculum, one in which students generated the ideas to be used in the classroom, one in which students taught each other through cross-teaching techniques, one in which the emphasis was on student cooperation and collaboration.

The man was obviously a kook. Wouldn't my kids hoot and take advantage of the ensuing chaos? Wouldn't they tear each other up much worse than in their daily battles on the playground and in the halls? Terms like *cooperation* and *collaboration* weren't part of their vocabulary. And as for their teaching each other, wouldn't it be a case of the blind leading the blind? They didn't know a comma from a semiquaver.

I dismissed Moffett's ideas as preposterous; that is, until things at school became rather desperate. I finally decided to try the "Moffett way" because I didn't have anything to lose, and at least I thought I'd have the grim satisfaction of proving the man wrong.

Starting Out

The seventh graders were attempting to get through Alexander Key's science-fiction novel *The Forgotten Door.* Instead of doing my usual teacher monologue (euphemistically called "a class discussion"), I borrowed some activities involving group learning and collaboration from Moffett's handbook on language activities (1968a) and added others from various language arts experts.

I gave each small group a detailed task assignment related to *The Forgotten Door:* choosing a scene from the novel and revamping it as a Readers Theatre offering; creating movie advertisements of "coming attraction" trailers, involving highlights—as if the novel had been filmed; scripting the trial scene near the end of the novel; creating a tabletop model of the utopian world from which the hero comes; reporting on mind reading (the unusual talent of the main character); or improvising "what if" situations that would change the story's outcome, the theme, and the nature of the characters.

When the youngsters learned the new order of the day—collaborative learning, working in groups of five or six on different projects—they were very suspicious. However, the change of routine did make them more alert and wary, as if perhaps some nasty trick were about to be played upon them. But at least the glazed looks were gone.

Getting into It

The first few days were rough on all of us.

Some youngsters were upset by the bedlam and noise; others reveled in it, just messing about. Some refused to work with their classmates; others gave up because they wanted hard-and-fast answers rather than tentative explorations. There existed mistrust not only between the racial factions within the room but between the boys and girls. Often ridicule, "jivin'," teasing, and tension would build within a group and boil over into confrontation.

I learned quickly that collaborative learning does not magically happen. You have to set up conditions carefully, and you have to allow time for both youngsters and teacher to make mistakes. Both have to adjust to a new series of demands put upon them, particularly the learning of cognitive and social skills that intertwine in a highly complex fashion.

Although I was tempted to abandon collaborative learning altogether, I didn't want to lose face in front of the youngsters and admit that I didn't know what I was doing. So I stuck it out. And I'm glad that I did, for as I floundered my way through, I tucked in the back of my mind some basic principles that eventually helped me make collaborative learning work effectively.

My worst assumption: the teacher's job is to set up detailed tasks for the students and then stand back while the students complete the assigned tasks on their own, with all students, of course, being productively engaged during each day's fifty-minute period.

I didn't realize that in collaborative learning situations the teacher is constantly on the move: monitoring the group's progress, offering advice if the youngsters seem confused or stuck, suggesting alternatives if student plans go awry, demonstrating how to behave as a contributing member of the group, and taking care of behavioral problems. In other words, the teacher assumes a very active role in collaborative learning and, oftentimes, an exhausting one.

I also mistakenly assumed that the students would respond favorably to their assigned tasks; after all, the tasks had been recommended in glowing terms by Moffett and other high-powered names in language arts. The activities should have struck an enthusiastic chord in each student's breast.

Instead, members of the class were incensed, and they grumbled about having to do all of those "dumb assignments." They demanded to know what their immediate payoff would be "by doing that junk."

After consulting with some experienced elementary teachers about group work, I hastily revamped my strategies.

Starting Over

During the first session, which lasted no more than fifteen or twenty minutes rather than the entire fifty-minute class session, we explored the purpose of each group project. If it didn't make sense to the youngsters, the project was modified to suit the group's ideas. It became *their* project, not mine, thus becoming a real collaboration among students and between the students and the teacher.

I also let it be known that we would perform or demonstrate the projects—if they were good enough—before an eighth-grade class or perhaps even at a school assembly or maybe a PTA meeting. Now the youngsters had a *real* audience to consider, not just a hodge-podge of tasks to take up class time and to please the teacher.

During the second short session, I introduced the concept of brainstorming and set up basic rules for the youngsters to follow: (1) generate as many ideas off the top of your head as possible—the wilder the better; (2) avoid evaluating or justifying any of the ideas offered, and refrain from telling others that their ideas are "real stupid"; and (3) record every idea presented, even if some are repetitious.

Once each group had chosen a recorder, the group brainstormed possible ways of approaching their project.

During the next several short sessions—never more than ten to twenty minutes at a time—each group:

1. Chose its leader.
2. Fashioned an agenda of what was to be accomplished from the records kept during the brainstorming session.
3. Determined completion dates for the various components of the project.
4. Delegated responsibilities for each member of the group.
5. Determined how the project and each group member were to be evaluated.

These sessions didn't always go smoothly. The youngsters made mistakes as they learned to accept each other's ideas and to work together cooperatively and productively.

I made mistakes, too. I often tried to push the students too hard before they really had learned how to cooperate, assume responsibility, and work as a team.

My major roles were to keep each group on task, make sure that their ideas worked for them, and ensure that the final payoff would be a successful project and a good learning experience. The hardest part was being available when really needed but not doing tasks that the students could do for themselves.

Somehow or other, we completed the projects and exhibited/performed them before the highly critical eighth-grade class, with a few parents and the school principal also in attendance. My class seemed very pleased with the results, especially that of "shining" before their superiors, the eighth graders. They immediately wanted to know when they could do collaborative projects again. It was "neat-o stuff."

To use the old cliché, nothing breeds success like success. Both the youngsters and I were in a state of euphoria, so we confidently launched into a writing workshop, again borrowing ideas from James Moffett. Why tamper with success?

The Workshop Experience

In the workshop approach to writing, the student scribbles down whatever comes to mind for ten or fifteen minutes each day for a week or so. The scribbles might consist of a jumble of memories, current gripes, or hopes for the future. The student pays no attention to organization, development, or mechanics while spilling onto paper whatever comes to mind. These raw data are filed each day in the student's writing folder, which becomes, in essence, a "language bank" for possible future themes or projects. One distinct advantage of this approach is that "natural topics" (Moffett's term) emerge from the students' interest, experience, and perspective (as opposed to teacher-generated topics being imposed on them).

When enough data are collected in the writing folders, the students gather in informal groups of four or five. Each group combs the individual member's folder for interesting ideas that have potential for further development. Through a series of short group meetings, each student selects one idea from his or her folder and develops that germ idea into a theme. The group serves as an audience as well as a counseling service. The writer receives immediate feedback from the group on points that aren't clear or parts that need to be reorganized or further developed.

Within each workshop group, it is advantageous to place several youngsters who have editorial skills and who can help with mechanical problems as questions arise. Throughout the workshop's operations, the emphasis is on student cooperation and "cross-teaching"— that is, students helping and teaching each other.

I hate to admit this, but I found that often the youngsters within a group did a better job of explaining how to solve a particular problem than I could have. They seemed to understand each other's lingo better and provide more empathy.

During these sessions, I noticed that the groups worked more productively and with less friction than during our initial venture with *The Forgotten Door*. I could see that most of the students had made at least some progress in learning how to pool ideas and how to cooperate and help rather than be destructive and competitive.

They listened somewhat better, were a bit more courteous toward each other, and generated some enthusiasm about their schoolwork. On rare occasions, they were tolerant of and generous toward each other.

We read some of the finished papers aloud, duplicated others, and displayed some on the bulletin board. I was impressed with the quality of the papers, most of which were more vivid than papers generated from topics I had assigned. The topics ranged from a chocolate pudding fight at camp to the shooting of rats to a haunting exposition on how to survive when the gas heat is turned off because of nonpayment of utility bills.

It was at this point that I made my next mistake. I fell in love with collaborative learning as a means of student learning. Because the class had had success in using it twice, I saw group collaboration as the ultimate solution to all of my teaching problems.

Groups and the Limits of Grouping

We did *special needs* grouping for those who needed help with particular skills, such as dictionary skills, following directions, and finding the main ideas in paragraphs. We did *tutorial* groupings, in which youngsters with expertise served as advisors on mechanical skills while others lent their expertise on fashion, sports, stamps and coins, soap operas, and so on. We did *interest* groupings, in which some youngsters explored their hobbies or entertainment preferences while others put on a one-act melodrama, *Sorry, Wrong Number.*

Furthermore, we did *invitational* groupings, with the youngsters inviting members of other groups to join their group for drill games in language skills and for interdisciplinary science/language arts projects. We did *social* groupings, in which the students learned parliamentary procedure and came up with language arts games and activities for our Friday afternoon club. And we did *research* groupings for special reports and for conducting treasure hunts among the school library's reference materials.

I was so caught up in my love affair with grouping and collaboration that I didn't catch faint signals that the kids were beginning to tire of so much group work. However, with louder rumbles of discontent, it dawned on me that perhaps I was overdoing the collaborative learning bit.

I remember George, a small but feisty seventh grader. He shook his head in disgust and groused, "This is the groupingest class I was ever in."

Since that time, I've learned that although collaborative learning is a very effective means of instruction, I must use it sparingly, alternating it with whole-class activities, the buddy system, and individual activities.

I have come to know what the ancient Greeks meant by "the golden mean": they wisely believed in a balanced life, one not given over to any excesses. The same may be said of educational practices.

Although some educational gurus try to sell *the* way in their books and lectures, experienced teachers know that a mix, a *variety* of practices, is a sounder policy. The aphorism "Different strokes for different folks" certainly holds true here.

Some activities lend themselves well to collaborative learning; others call for an individual or whole-class approach. Moreover, some people work best in groups; others prefer to go it alone. Over the years, these two basic principles have guided my planning of language arts work, whether for fifth graders, junior/senior high schoolers, college undergrads/grads, or doctoral students.

As a rule of thumb today, I usually begin with whole-class work—the reading of a short story, for instance. We'll break into groups, sometimes having each group explore an assigned issue or value within the story; at other times, the groups ferret out for themselves the issues presented or the theme of the story, using their own experiences and insights as resources. Then we may do individual projects, such as writing assignments or journal reaction papers. And later we may conclude by forming panels or roundtables and try to reach a consensus on particular issues, or do some creative dramatics and videotape key scenes, or create analysis grids whereby comparisons and contrasts are made between the current story and those previously read.

For the teacher who has never tried collaborative learning but who might be tempted, I heartily recommend *Classroom Collaboration*, by Phillida Salmon and Hilary Claire (1984). Observing four classroom teachers who used different collaborative learning techniques and activities, Salmon and Claire report on the pros and cons of collaborative learning and give detailed examples of activities that work well. I can only wish that I had had such a book when I started. Such advice would have saved me many a headache and disaster.

References

Key, A. 1986. *The Forgotten Door.* New York: Scholastic Inc.

Moffett, J. 1968a. *A Student-Centered Language Arts Curriculum, Grades K–13: A Handbook for Teachers.* Boston: Houghton Mifflin Co.

———. 1968b. *Teaching the Universe of Discourse.* Boston: Houghton Mifflin Co.

Salmon, P., and H. Claire. 1984. *Classroom Collaboration.* London: Routledge & Kegan Paul.

3 Interactive Learning in the Composition Classroom

Caryl Klein Sills
Monmouth College
West Long Branch, New Jersey

The word *cooperation* means to act jointly, to concur; in other words, the individuals involved come to some kind of agreement. However, it is probable that a certain amount of dissension will have preceded consensus. It is within the tension of this initial opposition that learning takes place; cooperative learning is thus a deliberate attempt to take advantage of differing perspectives through the interaction of individuals and their ideas in a reciprocal or alternating action.

We might liken this view of interactive learning to a game of catch in which a ball is tossed randomly from individual to individual until the game, by mutual consent, is over. In interactive learning, an idea is tossed from individual to individual. Analogies aside, however, any discussion of group learning must first identify the advantage of this mode of learning compared with all other modes of learning. For example, in a 1983 study, Johnson and Johnson concluded that "working collaboratively with classmates, compared with learning individualistically or competitively, increases the positiveness of students' mood states, thereby increasing their motivation to achieve" (cited in Johnson and Johnson 1986, p. 12).

In this view, collaborative learning is dependent on the *positive* interdependence of group members, which contributes to the achievement of a common goal. Specifically, "students put into groups are only students grouped and are not collaborators, unless a task that demands consensual learning unifies the group activity" (Wiener 1986, p. 55). Therefore, teachers must foster positive attitudes in group members that will result in interactive and productive group learning.

Fostering Positive Interaction in Peer Response Groups

Before students can hold positive attitudes toward peer workshops in which group members' compositions are critiqued, teachers themselves must be convinced that peer-group evaluation of writing assignments will help students improve as writers; that is, that cooperative group learning will translate into better writing by the majority of the group's members. The most eloquent arguments for peer writing workshops come from Kenneth Bruffee and Peter Elbow.

According to Bruffee (1980),

> The basic idea of collaborative learning is that we gain certain kinds of knowledge best through a process of communication with our peers. What we learn best in this way is knowledge involving judgment. We can sit by ourselves and learn irregular French verbs, benzine rings, the parts of an internal combustion engine, or the rhetorical devices which are useful in eloquent or effective prose. But when we want to know how to use this discrete knowledge—to speak French, to combine organic compounds, to find out why an engine won't start and then to fix it, or actually to write eloquent prose—we have to learn quite differently. . . .
>
> The best way to learn to make judgments is to practice making them in collaboration with other people who are at about the same stage of development as we are. (p. 103)

Elbow (1973) conceives of a teacherless writing experience in groups of seven to twelve people in which "everyone reads everyone else's writing. Everyone tries to give each writer a sense of how his words were experienced" (p. 77). Elbow further explains that it is often necessary for the writer to see his or her words and thoughts "refracted" through a reader's consciousness in order to use language that more clearly communicates the intended meaning: "To improve your writing you don't need advice about what changes to make; you don't need theories of what is good and bad writing. You need movies of people's minds while they read your words" (p. 77).

Thus, according to Elbow, the advantage to writers of having real readers is to provide immediate feedback. Adapting Elbow's teacherless writing groups in a traditional composition class means that although the teacher remains in the background while the groups operate, he or she, according to Wiener, is "neither inactive nor nondirective." In fact, to ensure productive collaboration the teacher "must plan and organize the session so that students know that the end is not simply to work in groups but to work in groups in an effort to reach consensus for an important task" (1986, p. 61). In a composition class, this task is for students to respond to each other's writing and to revise and improve their own writing.

It is not enough, however, for the teacher alone to be enthusiastic about writing workshops. Once teachers become convinced that peer writing workshops are an effective tool for improving student writing, they must develop in their students the positive attitudes requisite to productive group learning. Although students should be left pretty much on their own to read and respond to each other's writing, the following ways to structure peer groups will promote positive interaction between group members to ensure them a productive learning experience.

Structures for Peer Writing Workshops

In one model for peer-group response, the same task is assigned to each group: read and respond to each group member's writing. Then each group's findings, as well as the process that led them to their conclusions, are shared in a whole-class "wrap-up." Alternatively, each group can be assigned one part of a task. For example, different groups can critically evaluate the content, form, language, and sentence structure of a sample student essay and then report their findings for synthesis by the whole class (which then functions as a larger cooperative learning group). This sharing of information and experience by individual groups with the class as a whole is an important complement to small-group cooperative learning.

Written evaluation of each individual's group experience should be handed in for teacher comment but not for grading. Whenever possible, the instrument for this evaluation should be designed by the class as a whole after the task has been defined by the teacher. Specific points should be addressed, such as "What questions has the writer raised but not answered?" and "What is the focus of the essay, and is it consistent throughout?" Questions specific to a particular writing assignment might include "How does the writer concede or refute opposing arguments?" or "Does the writer provide sufficient explanations to connect the sequenced steps or stages of the process analysis?" General comments on the group experience and possible follow-through should also be solicited. For example, students might consider what revisions they will make after the group discussion, what their main contribution was to the critical discussion of others' writing, or how the workshop was either helpful or disappointing.

Students will often require instruction in interpersonal and small-group skills before they can successfully cooperate in peer response groups. The collaborative skills students need to use include leadership, communication, trust building, and conflict management skills (Johnson and Johnson 1986). During the wrap-up discussion at the end of each workshop session, the teacher can reinforce students' understanding of how to effectively use these skills by focusing on successful strategies reported by another group. For example, if a student feels his or her group is making only superficial comments, such as "That's real good" or "I like your introduction," members of other groups can be asked to suggest how they successfully solicited more useful feedback. In addition, the teacher can demonstrate how a writer can probe such surface responses with specific questions, such as "What is the least interesting part of my essay? What is lacking?" or "What expectations does my introduction set up for the reader? How can I fulfill them?"

A final way to ensure productive learning groups is to define responsibilities clearly. Both the writing assignment and the directions for group cooperation should be written out. In addition, leadership can be rotated at each workshop session, or group members can share authority to arrive at consensual decisions about procedures.

The most important point about peer-response writing groups is that in order to be motivated to achieve a productive group experience, students need to understand exactly what they are being asked to do, how they should go about doing it, when the assignment is to be completed, and what the individual benefits are likely to be. As we would expect, after a student receives an improved grade on a piece of writing that group members have responded to, he or she will be eager to participate in future workshops. As a result, both the teacher's goal of improved writing and the student's goal of improved grades become one unified, achievable goal.

Collaborative Writing

Students can also be grouped to collaboratively plan, draft, and revise a writing assignment for a common grade. The following three models are appropriate to this group learning experience:

1. The responsibility for drafting specific parts of a writing assignment, planned by the group as a whole, is delegated to individuals. The group then collaborates to revise and edit the parts into a single coherent whole.

2. Each member of the group writes a first draft of the whole assignment, which has been jointly planned by the group. All of the drafts are responded to and commented on by the group. A synthesis is arrived at consensually by the group members, who then revise and edit the final copy in concert.

3. A group of writers sits together and plans, drafts, and revises a piece of writing, which thus becomes a single response to the assignment.

In all three models, the group accepts joint responsibility for the planning and revising of the final product; only the drafting process affords alternatives.

Certainly, some writing assignments are more conducive to group collaboration than others. The following are two assignments that have worked particularly well—the first in freshman composition and the second in a business writing course.

Students in the freshman composition course were formed into groups to decide on a common grievance experienced within or outside the college. Individuals were responsible for gathering information from interviews, observations, questionnaires, and print or film sources. They pooled this information and drafted a report on the problem and its solution following any one of the procedural models presented above. Typical grievances included inadequate on-campus parking, course registration complexities and delays, drinking-age restrictions at campus functions, and harassment of teenaged drivers by local police.

The business writing students collaborated on a sales letter/promotion for a hypothetical new restaurant. Groups in this class wrote an assumption sheet that covered (1) the target market and why it was chosen, (2) the "vital statistics" of the proposed restaurant (type, location, decor, etc.) and why it would appeal to the target market, and (3) a description of any enclosures (brochures, coupons, consumer testimonials, etc.) that would be included with the letter and why they would be effective supplements. Both the assumption sheet and the final copy of the sales letter were collaboratively written, with each group choosing to follow one of the three procedural models described above.

Both assignments received a single grade, which was shared by all the members of a group. After the assignments were completed, each student evaluated the group experience in writing, including an analysis of his or her own and others' contributions. For the students, these written evaluations put the cooperative writing experience into perspective as a useful tool for both academic and career goals. For the teacher, the evaluations afforded a basis for evaluating individual performance within the group so that interaction among group members could become even more productive in future cooperative projects.

Understandably, some teachers are uncomfortable and, therefore, reluctant to give students a grade in common for a collaboratively written assignment because the input by each individual will doubtless be uneven. However, there are two excellent reasons not to shy away from assigning a shared grade for cooperative projects: (1) the collaboratively written assignment is just one grade out of many that will determine an individual's final grade for the course and, therefore, probably will not unduly influence the final grade; and (2) the ability to function effectively as part of a team is a marketable skill in both the academic world and the business world. For example, business reports are frequently a collaboration between departments and individuals; academic research studies are just as often a joint venture and the resultant articles necessarily coauthored. Therefore, students need to experience group cooperation first in an instructional environment so that they can learn to effectively use small-group skills and interpersonal skills. Human progress has been as much a record of group effort as it has been a consequence of individual genius. Everyone needs to learn to work productively in groups; writers are no exception.

Criteria for Forming Interactive Learning Groups

For both peer response and collaborative writing groups, I have found that the optimum number of students is four or five. However, pairing students to respond to each other's writing early in the semester is helpful as an introduction to the group experience. Some pairs can switch partners to keep the activity productive for those who progress more quickly through the assignment. Larger groups can be formed once the students are comfortable working in twos or threes.

Whether the groups are formed by the students' choice, randomly assigned (such as by counting off), or assigned by the teacher is a matter of the instructor's goals. Self-chosen groups might be more motivating for some individuals who find it important to be with friends or with those whom they perceive as potentially friendly. Assigned groups can be either homogeneous—grouped by major field of study or interest in a particular topic—or heterogeneous, with writers of varying skills or interests. Groups formed by random selection prevent any prejudicial influence by either the teacher or the students.

However, to effectively develop mutual trust and genuine two-way communication, the groups in a composition class should remain stable for at least half a semester (a whole semester is preferable). Again, the teacher's goals and assessment of the productivity of the groups would be the deciding factors in how often the groups should re-form. There is really no prescription that fits every situation.

A Word about Computers

Increasingly, composition courses are being taught on the computer, which affords a wonderful opportunity to introduce both collaborative writing and peer response groups. Because one's writing is readily viewable on-screen, computers foster social interaction as compared with the private (and often lonely) experience of pen-and-paper composing. Therefore, students can comfortably interact first on an informal, one-to-one basis before being assigned to a specific group. We have only to take advantage of this "openness" of computer-assisted composing to encourage a positive attitude toward cooperative learning.

My own experience using peer response groups and assigning collaborative writing has convinced me that cooperative learning groups promise the most effective and enjoyable model for teaching writing. We would do well to heed Peter Elbow's observation: "There is a profound principle of learning here: we can learn to do alone what at first we could do only with others" (1981, p. 190).

References

Bruffee, K. A. 1980. *A Short Course in Writing*. 2nd ed. Boston: Little, Brown.

Elbow, P. 1973. *Writing without Teachers*. New York: Oxford University Press.

———. 1981. *Writing with Power*. New York: Oxford University Press.

Johnson, D., and R. Johnson. 1983. The Socialization and Achievement Crisis: Are Cooperative Learning Experiences the Solution? In *Applied Social Psychology Annual 4*. Beverly Hills, Calif.: Sage.

———. 1986. Computer-Assisted Cooperative Learning. *Educational Technology* 26 (January): 12–18.

Wiener, H. S. 1986. Collaborative Learning in the Classroom: A Guide to Evaluation. *College English* 48: 52–61.

4 The Power of Collaboration

Carol Gilles
University of Missouri

Marc VanDover
Jefferson Junior High School
Columbia, Missouri

The television news and the newspaper had both reported the United States' attack on Libya. By noon the junior high students had heard about it. Five seventh graders burst into their classroom trailer and the discussion began:

Jane: We need to discuss this!

Diana: Please, let us talk about it!

Other voices joined the chorus. The teacher, Marc VanDover, sighed, "There go the lesson plans." He drew a map of Libya and the "Line of Death" on the board; a spirited discussion began. The students decided to express their opinions in a letter to President Reagan. They talked about how the letter should be organized, and each student wrote a part of it. They consolidated the parts of the letter and critiqued it. Then the students revised their shared letter, questioning themselves about the clarity of their stated intentions. They asked the teacher to type a final copy and to mail it.

Observers of this group might conclude that this is a class of academically talented and gifted students who are considering current events. These are the students who can discuss issues, make decisions, and use both their interests and the processes of reading and writing. It *couldn't* be a class for learning-disabled students—but it is.

From the research literature, we know that learning-disabled students have difficulty reading, do not do well in school, may drop out or get in trouble with the law, are not as popular as non-disabled classmates (Bryan 1974), "emit and receive more rejection statements than non-disabled classmates" (Bryan and Bryan 1978, p.

33)—the list goes on and on. The literature states little about what learning-disabled students *can* do.

In the classroom described above, collaboration provides the framework that allows students to show what they can do. This seventh-grade resource room is a place where students labeled learning-disabled can improve their reading, writing, and math processes while receiving support with their mainstream coursework. Collaboration invites students to be decision makers. As they discuss and make plans, students practice not only their linguistic and cognitive skills but their social skills as well. Reading and writing are used to solve real problems, and students soon see the necessity and the power of literacy. In such authentic settings, students are more willing to invest the time and effort needed to become proficient readers and writers.

Observations on the Collaboration Process

Yetta Goodman (1978) stated that teachers can learn *about* students *from* students. This is done by carefully observing what they say and do. Such direct information both informs theory and improves practice. The following principles emerged from careful observation of the teacher and students described above as they engaged in the collaborative process.

1. Collaboration works best when students are given a real problem to solve.

When a contrived curriculum is applied to students, there can be little honest discussion, problem solving, or collaboration. Students must feel ownership in the collaborative process.

For example, the classroom for VanDover's students is housed in a trailer. One cold February day, the teacher stopped class by saying,

> I know we need to work on revising our whale letters, but I think we have a more immediate problem. The problem is those cars that park so close to the trailer. I noticed lots of you had trouble getting in the door today. I nearly had to climb over the cars. What should we do?

Leaving the question open, VanDover invited a response. Jeff suggested throwing eggs at the cars; Jane recommended dumping coffee grounds on them. Everyone had a good laugh, and then Jane suggested putting signs on the cars. The students discussed the merits of "Don't Park Here" versus polite messages that would congratulate those who hadn't parked so close to their classroom trailer. The group decided to remind those who had parked too close to the trailer not to do so. After agreeing on the appropriate types of signs and the tools needed for lettering, they set to work. The students consulted one another on appropriate spellings because, as Mary quietly explained to the teacher, "We want the people to be able to read them." When the signs were finished, they read each other's signs, added finishing touches, and posted them.

Making signs was a way to solve a problem that required written language that was meaningful to the students. The process of constructing the signs required writing (composing, revising, and editing), reading (both one's own sign and others' signs), and problem solving through talking and listening. These students proved to themselves that in our society people can express their concerns through writing.

2. A collaborative environment grows slowly.

A collaborative environment is nurtured by a teacher who considers everyone to be a resource, who allows risks to be taken and mistakes to be made, and who doesn't always have "the right answer."

VanDover views his classroom as a place where students practice solving problems. He often begins class by reading aloud an article dealing with a topic or a problem that would be engaging to his students—year-long school, the endangered whales, X-ratings on rock music. He invites discussion, and often he asks students to do a freewriting concerning how they feel about the issue. If some students choose to do more with the topic, he allows that choice and acts as a resource for their project.

Everyone in VanDover's room is a resource person. At the beginning of the year when students asked a question, VanDover would often wait before responding. During that wait time, it became common to hear another student say, "I could help her with that." VanDover encourages students to consult one another when they have questions, and if they still need help to come to him. Without abdicating authority, he makes it clear that everyone in the room has certain abilities and talents that can be tapped.

VanDover demonstrates to students that he is a learner and that they can be teachers. He shares books he loves and pieces of his own writing. He invites students to teach the class. In order to assume the role of teacher, the students decide what to teach, prepare lesson plans, check the plans with VanDover, and then instruct the class.

They often reflect their teacher's practices. For example, two students-turned-teachers included sustained silent reading in their plans; the class regularly read silently or listened as the teacher read to them. However, unlike VanDover's regular practice, both students moved around the classroom during the reading time instead of reading. This disrupted the other students' reading, and the lessons that followed were less than successful. After the second student-teacher finished, VanDover talked with the class about what he'd learned from the lesson. He said, "Watching you made me think of things that I'm not doing. I don't stop growing or learning just because I'm the teacher. By watching you I see that if I assign reading, I should do it. If I assign writing, I should do that, too." After that day, whenever students wrote in their journals or read silently, VanDover joined them.

3. Collaboration isn't a panacea.

Collaboration is not immune to problems. In fact, working through these problems is a part of collaboration that helps make the classroom a community. For example, the first time one student taught, she jumped from topic to topic, asked students to read, interrupted their reading, and switched assignments. It was a disaster. Students were restless during her lesson and obviously unhappy. Instead of interrupting her lesson, however, VanDover chose to have the students discuss the experience:

> *VanDover:* I think we can really learn from each other if we do this. And I'd like to go on and try it again, if anyone wants to be the teacher. But what I want to know as a group, what can we do differently? How did we react to Jane's being the teacher?
>
> *Mary:* Very silly.
>
> *VanDover:* Why?
>
> *Diana:* Because she wasn't a good teacher. [Looking at Jane] Sorry.
>
> *Jeff:* She didn't teach us anything. She could teach us more.
>
> *VanDover:* Okay, what do you want to do differently?
>
> *Jeff:* Well, maybe if we act more like students, she'll act more like a teacher. No more goofing off.
>
> *Diana:* Maybe she could teach us something like she learned in Science or World Cultures.

The discussion continued as students brainstormed ways of making the "teacher of the day" experience richer and more meaningful to them.

They had learned that as members of a community, they could not expect all the activities they initiated to work; but as they worked through problems, they became more responsible for their own parts in the learning process. Dewey (1938) wrote that schooling must reflect real life. Real life has problems and obstacles. Letting students work through problems encountered in the collaboration process—instead of the teacher identifying the problem, making the decision, and administering disciplinary action—helps students to prepare for real life.

4. Students do not have to be directly involved in the collaboration to learn from it.

Frank Smith (1983) believes that we learn vicariously. That is, when we are engaged with some person's demonstration, we learn from it. Dorothy Watson insists we learn 80 percent of what we know by eavesdropping (personal communication, 14 June 1986). If students are interested and engaged, even those on the periphery of the learning event can benefit from the event.

In VanDover's class, Amy seemed to have severe problems. She often worked on math assignments during class and rarely participated in class discussions. However, when she was interviewed, Amy indicated that she had both understood and remembered many of the discussions and activities initiated by class members. Amy's understanding of current events and problem solving had grown because of her presence in the class, even though there were few demands on her to participate overtly.

Jeff is another example. When asked if he learned anything from classmates, he responded, "Well, I was listening to Mary help Amy. I was listening to them 'cause I was waiting for Mr. VanDover, and I learned a little bit about different sorts of angles." He went on to explain obtuse, acute, and right angles—a unit his math teacher had not yet covered. When students are interested, engaged in the demonstration, and free from the fear of failing, they can and do learn from one another.

Conclusion

VanDover's classroom is a community of language users. As in any community, there are decisions to be made, meanings to be negotiated, and tasks to be completed. The process of collaboration invites students to become more facile language users and more confident in their interpersonal relations. As special education students learn that they can be decision makers, they gain confidence and are less dependent on the teacher.

This self-reliance was illustrated one day when VanDover was absent. The class had decided earlier to write to Huynh Quang, the author of *The Land I Lost,* a book VanDover had read to them. The substitute teacher asked students to brainstorm what needed to be included in the letter. She recorded their comments on the board, often abandoning their linguistic preferences for her own. The discussion dragged, and finally Jane could stand it no more. She stood up and announced, "Oh, I know what should go next!" She grabbed some chalk and motioned to her classmates for support.

To her credit, the substitute teacher sat down. The tenor changed. When the students realized this was *their* letter, ideas were plentiful and Jane dutifully and accurately recorded them. The students regarded the substitute as a resource person and solicited her ideas on spellings, correct closings, and standard grammar. The letter was finished just before the bell rang. Was the substitute teacher angry? After all, the students had taken her lesson and made it their own. As they filed out, she sighed, "I've never been in a class where the students wanted so much to learn. And there are no points, no names on the board . . ." Her voice trailed off, and she shook her head. "If all classes were like this, subbing would be a pleasure."

When students use collaboration to take control of their own schooling, *learning* is a pleasure, too.

References

Bryan, T.H. 1974. Peer Popularity of Learning Disabled Children. *Journal of Learning Disabilities* 7: 621–25.

Bryan, T.H., and J.H. Bryan. 1978. Social Interactions of Learning Disabled Children. *Learning Disability Quarterly* 1: 33–38.

Dewey, J. 1938. *Experience and Education.* New York: Collier Books.

Goodman, Y. 1978. Kid Watching: An Alternative to Testing. *National Elementary Principal* 57, no. 4: 41–45.

Smith, F. 1984. *Essays into Literacy.* Exeter, N.H.: Heinemann.

5 Fine Cloth, Cut Carefully: Cooperative Learning in British Columbia

Tom Morton
Prince of Wales Secondary School
Vancouver, British Columbia

Teachers can structure student interaction in three principal ways. First, like Rocky Balboa in the ring, students can compete in a classroom to see who is best; when the bell curve rings, they are there to win or lose. Second, teachers can require students to work individually, like long-distance runners. As with Lily Tomlin's wry paradox, they're all in this . . . alone. Lastly, teachers can organize their class into small groups to work interdependently and collaboratively to master the assigned material. Like mountain climbers scaling a curricular mountain, they succeed or fail together.

In British Columbia, competitive and individualistic teaching techniques dominate our pedagogy, yet recently school boards, colleges, and teachers have shown increasing interest in cooperative strategies. For the last two years I have been involved with thirty other teachers in a program with David Johnson and Roger Johnson of the University of Minnesota. The material they have provided us is fine, cut carefully to the lessons of implementation research, and it is from this cloth that I have fashioned the approaches described here.

Elements of Effective Collaboration

For the Johnsons, cooperative learning is much more than putting students into groups. Effective collaboration must include four elements:

The first is positive interdependence. There must be a structure to ensure that the group works together. For example, I often assign a mutual goal such as a group report; at other times, I divide the assignment into different tasks or distribute different materials but

35

make each part necessary to complete the whole assignment. In addition, there can be different but complementary behavioral roles for each student, such as summarizer, encourager, or understanding checker. Joint rewards, such as a whole or partial group grade, free time, or privileges, also promote interdependence.

The second key element seems obvious to me, but many students still balk in the first few weeks when I ask them to sit "looking and facing each other" or, as the Johnsons say, "eye-to-eye and k-to-k" (knee to knee). (One useful approach to convince my senior students of the importance of seating is to show them diagrams of the various seating plans the United States and North Vietnam argued over for six months during the Vietnam War. Eight thousand Americans and many more Vietnamese died during those six months.)

The third key element is individual responsibility. The biggest complaint I used to get from students about group work was about the "hitchhiker," who goes along for the ride but doesn't contribute. I do not want to level the top students down but to bring the bottom ones up, so now, although the group learns in a collaborative manner, each student *must* be responsible for some task.

Fourthly, cooperative learning requires students to use appropriate interpersonal skills. Teachers should not assume that students know how to behave in groups. We need to teach that "how," starting with basic skills such as moving quickly and quietly to join one's group members, and progressing to more advanced skills such as paraphrasing. Then we need to monitor and support the use of these skills.

The Elements in Practice

In the first few weeks, I divide the class randomly into groups of three for cooperative lessons. Sometimes I ask them to number off—in English one day, French or Chinese another; at other times I ask for nine or ten famous authors and we "author off." The learning teams vary in composition early on so that the students have time to get to know a variety of classmates and so that I can evaluate their social skills for future grouping. In addition, the collaborative skills training is integrated with content lessons.

At the end of the month, I assign the students to heterogeneous groups on the basis of their social and academic skills levels. The selection ideally mixes students of different academic abilities, different social skills, different cultures, and different friendship groups.

My own experience and research support heterogeneity in trying to build a supportive climate and high academic standards. These teams become base groups for the majority of group projects for several months, though I will change them when necessary (for example, when I want to use student observers). The life of a group passes through several stages before a period of high productivity; therefore, in order for groups to reach the most rewarding level, the members need time to become comfortable with one another and to develop strategies for working together.

Reaching that level, where students accomplish a great deal and enjoy working together, requires much encouragement, practice, and coaching. The lesson structure—positive interdependence and individual responsibility—and the ability to use collaborative skills are key, but other approaches can help. I give pep talks, frequently refer to the rationale with examples from the work world, celebrate successes, and above all process group exercises. *Processing* means discussion after a lesson about how well the group did. Sometimes this can be fairly informal, such as when I ask the teams to discuss and write down their answers to two questions: "What did you do well in this lesson?" and "What could you do better next time?" At other times, I supply detailed evaluation sheets that ask for comments on who actively listened, who offered encouragement, and the like, as well as what could be improved. Observation sheets are important for providing feedback, which is often surprising to the students and which helps processing.

Group members sink or swim together. Evaluation may depend on a group result (for example, a single report on a topic or a single solution to a problem), or it may be individual but with bonus marks if all team members achieve a certain mark on a test. This interdependence is essential to ensure that the team works together, but it usually means too that in at least one group the majority will be vexed or disappointed at some point with someone who lets the group down. I respond quickly to this situation in three main ways: expand the processing to explore the reasons for failure and possible solutions, give extra coaching to individual students to make sure they succeed on the test or assignment, and negotiate different standards for success on an exam or different tasks for completion of an assignment.

Almost any content area can be tailored to a cooperative structure (although *Romeo and Juliet* was the hardest to plan, and a visit from the CBC National News to videotape a lesson on poverty was the scariest).

The trickster side of me leads my lessons to puzzles, games, and problem solving, such as a mystery to solve or an essay to piece together from jumbled sentences. For a mystery lesson, as developed by Gene Stanford (1977), each student is provided a card with one or more clues to read aloud but not to show to someone else or give away. There is one answer (requiring interdependence), and each member must be able to explain how to arrive at the answer (individual responsibility). The mystery structure can be used for many games—for example, a vocabulary exercise based on a study of eponyms, in which each student has a clue and the group has the task of guessing the eponym, as below.

Clues: 1. This word has three syllables.
           2. This word refers to a close-fitting garment.
           3. This noun is associated with dance.
           4. This word comes from a nineteenth-century French trapeze performer.

Answer: leotard

Clues: 1. Romeo's friend in *Romeo and Juliet* had a similar name and appropriate temperament.
           2. This word has the same origin as the name of one of the planets.
           3. This word comes from the Roman god of eloquence, skill, and thievery.
           4. This word is an adjective that means lively, witty, changeable, and quick-tempered.

Answer: mercurial

The same structure works well for a grammar game with the goal of constructing a single sentence and instructions like these:

1. Use the passive voice.

2. Use an appositive.

3. Use the present tense.

4. Use two verbs for your predicate.

For group assignments I prefer those that involve inventiveness and creativity and thus profit the most from the group process. One of my favorites with juniors follows from a reading of excerpts from Swift's "Rules That Concern Servants in General" and Woody Allen's "A Brief, Yet Helpful, Guide to Civil Disobedience." Using the list format, I ask groups to complete one of the following parodies of rules:

1. List the usually unstated rules for winning in hockey, basketball, politics, and other violent sports.
2. Give advice to admiring elementary school students on how to survive secondary school.
3. Create a foolproof plan on how to get an F or an A in this class.
4. Write a child's curriculum guide for educating parents, teachers, brothers and sisters, goldfish, vacuum cleaner salespersons, etc.

In the parody assignment, interdependence is increased by specific group roles: one student writes down ideas and the final product, a second checks for correct English, and the third reads the parody to the class. These roles can also be collaborative. Here is an example of a role description I've used from a Jefferson County, Colorado, science textbook (1982):

Summarizer

You are to restate the group's assignment as soon as the group meets. Keep the group's attention on the task. Check to make sure all members get a chance to give their ideas and participate. Restate the ideas expressed. Summarize the group decisions. Make sure every member has a job to do. In case of absences, divide absentee's job among members present. Check to make sure everyone agrees with group's decisions. When the work is done, get group members' signatures on the group product, signifying that they have helped with and approve the work. Be prepared to explain your group's product or decision and to describe how your group worked together. Also, it is your responsibility to use the group skills. (quoted in Johnson and Johnson 1984, p. 403)

For *Romeo and Juliet* I am obliged to walk through the play with my grade-11 classes first for initial comprehension. Then we use the jigsaw method developed by Elliot Aronson (1978) to deepen our understanding. Each learning team has an act for which they are to be the experts, and each student has an element of the act to analyze; more capable students have to look for theme and mood, and weaker ones describe the plot and character. Together the team members write up their descriptions with colored felt-tip pens on large posters and then teach the class. The poster format makes the analysis a proud decoration and a good study aid. Evaluation is based on a single final product.

Probably my most exciting, though most complex, cooperative lessons have been centered on controversial topics and structured on the Johnsons' (1982) model. I've developed lessons on topics such as the World War Two Canadian raid on Dieppe and U.S. investment in Canada, but my most controversial lesson involved conflicting images of British Columbia from a government booklet and a teachers' federation unit on poverty in the province. Both publications were hot political items and often in the news, so when the CBC National News tempted me with a siren call of fame, I agreed to let them tape my class.

The actual lesson structure is too long to explain fully here, but in brief, I assigned students into groups of four and divided them again into pairs, one for each side of the debate. Partway into the debate, the students had to switch sides and argue their opponent's previous position. In the end, the four worked together to write a single report on their opinion of our province.

Unfortunately, I have no sordid behind-the-camera stories to tell because less spellbound voices convinced me that in the charged climate the news story might be misinterpreted. I tied myself to the mast and canceled the taping. We had a great class, but the controversy stayed inside the classroom.

Conclusion

Despite all the mishaps—and implementing cooperative learning is not easy—my own experience, along with educational research from the University of Minnesota (Johnson, Johnson, and Johnson-Holubec 1986) and Johns Hopkins University (Slavin 1986), supports the advantages of cooperation compared to competition and individual work. A meta-analysis of 122 earlier studies (Johnson et al. 1981) strongly indicates higher performance, especially in higher-level complex tasks such as concept attainment and problem solving. In addition, cooperative learning promotes more positive attitudes toward the subject areas studied, greater competency in working with others, more respect for diversity, and greater perceptions of the grading system as fair.

Yet interesting educational innovations are like socks: they won't stand up unless a teacher wears them. Too often, textbooks or strategies are thrown to the teacher mismatched, the wrong size, and full of holes. Sometimes they only stand up because they are smelly and old. However, in the implementation program organized here by the Vancouver Association of Wholistic Education, the Vancouver School Board, and Douglas Community College, the material is well matched and well tailored to teacher needs, with released time for workshops, monthly meetings, support teams, and classroom coaching. New programs have also followed the success of the original thirty teachers.

The ideal of students sharing, supporting, and challenging each other in striving toward academic excellence is a powerful one. With the high-quality fabric of cooperative learning and a careful implementation design, in my classroom and those of other involved teachers, the ideal has increasingly become actualized in student practice.

References

Aronson, E., et al. 1978. *The Jigsaw Classroom*. Newbury Park, Calif.: Sage.

Johnson, D., and F. Johnson. 1982. *Joining Together: Group Theory and Group Skills*. Englewood Cliffs, N.J.: Prentice-Hall.

Johnson, D., and R. Johnson. 1984. *Cooperative Learning*. New Brighton, Minn.: Interaction.

Johnson, D., R. Johnson, and E. Johnson-Holubec. 1986. *Circles of Learning: Cooperation in the Classroom*. Edina, Minn.: Interaction.

Johnson, D., G. Maruyama, R. Johnson, D. Nelson, and L. Skon. 1981. Effects of Co-operative, Competitive, and Individualistic Goal Structures on Achievement: A Meta-Analysis. *Psychological Bulletin* 89: 47–62.

Pratt, H., and B. J. Meadows, coordinators. 1982. *Topics in Applied Sciences*. Jefferson County Public Schools, Colorado.

Slavin, R. 1986. *Using Student Team Learning*. Baltimore: Johns Hopkins University Press.

Stanford, G. 1977. *Developing Effective Classroom Groups*. New York: Hart.

6 A Writing Teacher's Guide to Processing Small-Group Work

E. Kathleen Booher
Old Dominion University

Many teachers have discovered great value in using peer writing groups in the classroom. However, some of us are concerned that students may not gain as much through the group experience as we would like. What teachers often feel they lack is processing (or debriefing) skills—strategies to promote their students' immediate examination of what they have just done in groups.

Most students are not yet capable of both extracting the purpose of their activity from their experience and evaluating their accomplishments. These are sophisticated skills. As professional educators, we can provide the structure within which our students can develop their abilities of self-examination.

In short, this is what a processing session is all about: it should invite students to contemplate what is happening to them as writers and as members of peer writing groups.

What Is Processing?

Processing is a teacher-led activity that immediately follows small-group work. The teacher assumes the role of facilitator, which involves questioning, suggesting, and directing the discussion. It helps if students are seated in a somewhat circular or horseshoe arrangement, individually or clustered in groups. The more eye contact each student can make with others in the entire group, the more likely they all will be to engage in dialogue rather than to speak only to the teacher.

What Should I Do?

As facilitator, you will select two or three key questions to focus the discussion. You might join your students by taking a chair in the circle. Or you could stand outside the circle, moving about and making eye contact with all. In a horseshoe arrangement, you might sit or stand in the opening. In either arrangement, standing communicates more teacher control over the activity, while sitting turns more of the control over to the students.

Because a major purpose of small-group processing is to encourage students to accept responsibility for their own learning, you can help your students most by working toward less teacher control. Your decisions about that, however, may vary from one class to another, from one age group to another, and even from one moment to the next during a single session. You may find, for instance, that if you stand early in the session, restless students settle down more quickly. Once discussion is under way, your taking a seat may go unnoticed and will not affect student dialogue.

How Long Should a Processing Session Last?

The answer could be two minutes, or twenty, or more—depending on your objectives and your students' ages and attention spans. In some activities you might want students to reassemble as a class for a feeling of closure or togetherness before the school day or class period ends. Working in small groups without even a brief return to the large group can bring feelings of fragmentation or incompleteness to the activity. For a short debriefing with young children, you might simply ask, "How many of you had a good idea today while you wrote? What good idea did you hear in your group that you'd like the entire class to hear?" Then, after one or two students have shared their ideas, that day's session could end.

What Questions Should I Ask?

Your questions will depend on many considerations: how experienced your students are as writers and small-group workers, what type of writing they're doing, what the small group was asked to accomplish, where you are in your instructional plans. The two or three questions you select will focus the ensuing discussions; therefore, you should develop questions that lead to the writing and sharing goals you have in mind. In any case, processing, like all educational experiences, should be approached *developmentally*. Design the processing so that it encourages students to (1) explore their writing and small-group behavior, (2) "own" what they discover about their behavior, and (3) act on these discoveries appropriately.

The following are some questions you might ask, depending on the developmental goals for your class(es):

To encourage students to gain control over their writing processes:

Was it easy or difficult to get started? Why?

Describe the moment you put pen to paper.

What happens to you *physically* while you write?

Do you reread and rewrite? How does that happen for you?

Did the time for writing seem long? Short?

Where does your writing seem to be going?

What do you do about planning throughout the process?

Did any of you make an outline? When? What does it look like?

When can you tell you're finished with a piece?

To encourage students to assume responsibility for their products:

What kinds of writing did you do today?

How much did you get to write in the time you had?

Does your writing today add up to something?

Has your writing arrived somewhere? Where?

Have you made it clear why you wanted to write the piece you're working on?

How can you find out if your piece said what you wanted it to?

What do you want to do with this writing?

To encourage students to consider their environmental needs *for writing:*

What writing tools do you like to use?

How would you describe your writing habits?

What sort of setting do you like for writing?

What can you do to help yourself write in the classroom?

At what time of day or night do you like to write?

How much time does "setting up" take?

To encourage students to acknowledge their attitudes *about writing:*

How did you feel when I asked you to write?

Does anyone feel anxious about getting started?

Can you describe how writing makes you feel?

What is it about writing that sometimes makes you anxious?

Which part of your piece brought you the most pleasure (or pain) as you wrote?

How did you feel when you read your piece?

Where do you think these feelings come from?

Why do many of us make apologies for our pieces before we read them?

How did you feel about the responses your group gave you today?

How does feeling angry (or afraid, happy, etc.) affect your ability to write?

To encourage students to develop good small-group working strategies:

What were some of the responses you received in your group today?

What are you doing when members of your group apologize before they read?

How can you include your groupmates who may not talk as much as you?

How do you make sure everyone gets to read?

How much of your group discussion was on track? Off track? Whose responsibility is that?

What do you do when all the members of your group think you need to write something differently?

Evaluation of Processing

How do you evaluate the success or failure of your processing efforts? Through results. If your students gradually show more interest in the process (their own and their peers'), if they assume increasing concern about the products they hand in, if they show courtesy for others while they write, if they talk openly about how writing makes them feel, and, finally, if they work more effectively in their groups as the semester wears on, then there is a very good chance that your processing time is working.

Remember, debriefing your students after small-group work, like writing, is a *process*. You get better at it the more you practice.

II Collaborative Learning and Literature Study

7 Cooperative Learning in the Literature Classroom

Rex Easley
University of Cincinnati

The English department at my university offers an "Introduction to Short Stories" course, which I suspect is much like introductory lit courses in English departments all over the country. Typically the class contains about thirty-five students, none of whom is in the humanities and all of whom are very grade-conscious. The students take the class because it fills a humanities slot in their overall graduation requirements. They come into the course expecting an easy grade and a passive learning situation—one which the instructor tells them what to know. Their background in literature is weak overall, and they usually bring to the class a negative attitude toward reading the "classics" of short fiction. They have already learned that literature, especially literature meant to be studied rather than enjoyed, consists of mysterious and boring writing that English teachers seem capable of reading a great deal into.

A course such as this is usually taught as a lecture/discussion, though *discussion* is probably an exaggeration. Stories are assigned and students come to class and listen to the "correct" interpretation of the story (some students attempt to answer the instructor's discussion questions, while most remain doggedly silent). Then on tests the students repeat this information, recorded in class notes and memorized the day before the test, to show the instructor what they've learned. And often what they've really learned is that the most successful students are those who are the best at guessing what the instructor wants to hear.

This situation, then, was the kind I found myself facing when I decided, after having taught the short story class in the traditional way for several years, that my students and I deserved something better. For one thing, I wanted them to gain a more meaningful access to the stories they read—to interact with each story instead of just studying it as an object. For another, I wanted their role in the class to be participatory, not passive. I wanted them to think for themselves instead of relying on me to tell them what to think. And as much as anything else, I wanted my students to *like* the stories they read and to find the course itself more pleasure than drudgery. But how was I to get a large group of passive grade-oriented non-majors who weren't even taking the course by choice to involve themselves wholeheartedly in the kind of exchange of ideas and responses that I envisioned?

The solution to that problem proved to be deceptively simple. I approached them through their biggest worry in the course—the essay tests. I knew from past experience that giving essay exams in a literature class can cause problems. Students complain of too little time and too much pressure, while teachers are usually disappointed because the students rarely deliver what the teacher really hopes for—ideas and insights that go beyond those given out by the teacher in class. Then it occurred to me that maybe I should have the literature students do what students in my composition classes were doing prior to writing; that is, working together in small groups to figure out what their topics required, deciding on an approach and something to say, helping each other, and learning from their conversations. As with a composition class, I would try to shift the emphasis from product to process.

At the start of the class time set aside for preparing for the first test, I gave the students the actual test questions. For each story on the exam, I devised a set of three questions that raised the kinds of issues I considered important for a reader's understanding of the story. I told the students that these were indeed the real test questions and that from each group of three I would choose one as *the* question for that story.

Before dividing the students into groups, I explained what acceptable answers would consist of. I said that I was open to any ideas that addressed the topic—even if those ideas didn't happen to agree with mine—so long as their views were supportable. I showed them, using several well-known examples, that critics disagreed with each other all the time. Thus, a "good" answer on the test would be one that they could make plausible by explaining what they were saying and backing up the ideas with specific references to the stories.

I presented this "new" approach under the guise of practical necessity: since there wasn't enough time to do both the thinking and the writing for these topics in one hour, I was giving them the chance to do the thinking in advance. And I suggested that while they were at it, here was a good opportunity to see if they were on the right track by comparing ideas and possible answers with each other—a comparison that might help them clarify their own understanding of each story. Then I put them into groups of four to six and handed out the test questions.

The first response was mild skepticism. Students asked if these were really the test questions or just "study hints," and one wanted to know if this was "all" they had to know about each story. Once in their groups, though, they showed a surprising willingness to try talking with each other—perhaps in part because I moved quickly from group to group to ensure that each made some kind of start, even if it was only having a group member read the first question aloud. Then I let the groups talk for a while, avoiding any participation myself except to answer the occasional request for clarification of the topics.

After each group had had enough time to get some tentative ideas out into the open, I began to sit in on first one group, then another, to get some sense of the direction of their discussion. When asked questions, I replied with another question—usually something like "Who goes along with that idea?" or "What would lead you to say that?" or simply "Why do you ask that question?" As they began to realize that I would not be providing answers, the questions became less frequent. Instead the group members found themselves trying to explain to each other where their ideas came from, and I would quietly move on to another group.

As I moved from group to group, I made an effort to encourage the students to trade ideas, question each other, and expect reasons for each other's views. I also suggested that they make notes to themselves and mark important passages on their own copies of the stories since they would be allowed to bring the copies with them to the exam—an additional incentive for them to listen to each other and to follow the discussion in their groups. Their responsibility, I said, was not to memorize the story but to know what they wanted to say about it.

The end of the class period found the groups in the middle of their discussions. They had more to say about the stories than they or I had imagined, and they wanted to continue—partly, I suspect, because they thought I was doing them a favor by letting them work together and because it was turning out to be a relatively painless way of "learning" the stories. So we pushed back the test, and when class met the next time the students went straight into their groups and took up where they had left off.

Over the next few weeks, all sorts of unexpected good things began to happen. As students got caught up in their exchange of ideas, enthusiasm for talking about the stories blossomed. It was not unusual for me to arrive at class early and find groups already well into their discussions in the hall. At the end of class I had difficulty in getting them to wrap things up and leave. I found more students wanting to talk with me before class, after class, and in my office, and usually they wanted to share a new idea or insight they'd just had. On test days they came in and wrote long well-developed essays, and the quality of the writing reflected what I believe was an increasing degree of confidence in what they had to say.

As the semester went along, more and more of our class time was given over to small-group discussion. The students began asking for the question list as soon as a new story was assigned, and I responded by giving them more questions per story. Then we talked over the whole list before choosing, by mutual consent, the three most important and interesting questions as the "official" test topics. I promoted a wider exchange of ideas by occasionally rotating half of each group to a new group and asking the new arrivals to summarize what their old group had to say about each question. And through it all I reminded them that they were free to say whatever they wanted as long as they could defend their views with explanation and examples.

It is probably clear by now that this class far exceeded any expectations I had at the start. By the end of the course, the students were routinely carrying on extended literary conversations that I think would be the envy of any graduate seminar in short stories, at least in terms of interest and participation. What they were looking for when they came into class was the easiest route to a good grade that they could find. What they got was an experience that seems to have changed their whole notion of their role as students. They learned to evaluate rather than take things on faith, and they learned that "right answers" don't have to come from the teacher—that their own responses are just as valuable as anyone else's. The students saw an underlying consistency in the way they all read and understood the stories, even in the midst of their interpretive disagreements, and this discovery gave them confidence in their integrity as readers. In doing all these things, they also came to realize some of the complexity and satisfaction of literary experiences for themselves.

Not losing sight of the original purpose of the collaborative learning groups was, I think, very important to the success of our efforts. The test-preparation format and rationale created both the means and the motivation for the students to pursue a common goal together. Their own success and pleasure in doing so led directly to a willingness to become even more involved with the stories and with their groups. So extensive and thorough were their discussions that the students eventually learned far more about each story and about how literature works than they ever could have learned in a lecture/discussion class. And best of all, they loved doing it.

8 Group Library Research and Oral Reporting in Freshman Composition

Barbara Schoen
State University of New York, College at Purchase

"But I would rather do the report by myself than with the group," Julia complains, detaining me after class.

"Learning to work with people is as important as learning how to do the report," I tell her.

"But suppose I do a lot of work and someone else . . ."

"Give it a try," I say, laying a hand on her arm. "I think you'll like this project."

She leaves, unconvinced.

Despite fears to the contrary, students *do* like this project. They enjoy the variety of tasks, and they understand that they are exercising research, reading, speaking, and writing skills. They are less aware that they are also learning both to work with other people and to manage an extended independent assignment.

The project fits naturally into the second semester of "Introductory Writing." After a semester of critical reading and writing centered on a single text, we move on to papers based on multiple sources—some of which require a library search. The project, which comes in the fifth week of the semester, consumes all or part of twelve class periods; the group part of the project occupies the first six.

The class, about twenty students, studies two plays: *The Crucible,* by Arthur Miller, an account of the Salem witch trials of 1692, and *Inherit the Wind,* by Jerome Lawrence and Robert E. Lee, a fictionalized version of the Scopes "Monkey" trial of 1925. The project has four parts:

1. Group preparation and library research on both trials (3–4 class periods)
2. Group oral reports on the library research (2–3 class periods)
3. Reading and discussion of plays (4 class periods)

4. A comparison and contrast paper on a major theme that is common to both plays

Since the focus of the present volume is collaborative learning, I will discuss only the first two parts of the project in detail.

At the start, I explain that we will be reading two plays and looking into their backgrounds. We develop methods and schedules. I add that, incidentally, it has worked well to do the library research and the oral reports in two study groups, one for each play. There are objections, both immediate and delayed.

I override the objections and ask for general information about either play. Most classes can volunteer both the locale and the central issues. I suggest that students look over the plays before the next class, at which time we will form study groups according to individual preferences.

"Sooo—," I say at the beginning of the next class, "before we choose our groups, let's talk about how to go about what we are going to do." I am deliberately vague. The class is temporarily nonplussed. The discussion might continue this way:

> *Student:* Well, we could go to the library and look up about the trials.
>
> *Teacher:* Good. What about the trials?
>
> *Student:* Who did something wrong.
>
> *Teacher:* [writing the suggestion on the board] Okay. What else?
>
> *Student:* What happened?
>
> *Teacher:* Fine. [writing] You mean like—the outcome? The punishment? [I am trying to move them to specifics.] What else happens at a trial?
>
> *Students:* Judges, juries, lawyers . . .
>
> *Teacher:* [writing fast] Are both trials about the same thing?
>
> *Class:* Witches, religion, evolution . . .
>
> *Teacher:* We'd better make separate lists, one for each trial.

They don't think of all aspects. I may have to digress on the McCarthy-era hearings, creationism, or other examples. We find a dozen or so topics for each trial. Each of these topics will generate a brief individual oral report.

After we have subdivided the general topic into specific ones, it is time to choose individual topics. "Who'd like to do what?" I ask, ready to write. Names attach to topics quickly: the groups are formed.

As an alternate procedure, groups can be chosen *before* developing specific topics; however, choosing *after* discussion helps ensure that interest in the topic will override interest in the group lineup. I form groups of equal size by carefully selecting which of the suggested topics I write on the board.

"Now," I tell them, "Let's get together with your groups. You can move your chairs around."

They chatter and, perhaps, suggest that the groups be named "Monkeys" and "Witches." I don't join either group, but move casually around the room. "Think about how to manage your presentation, now," I tell them.

Discussions begin:

"Who goes first in the group?"

"It has to make sense from the topics."

"We need to keep a list." Julia, who didn't want to work in groups, volunteers to be recorder.

"Suppose someone is sick."

They work through their preparations with little help from me—deciding on introductions, order of appearance, shifts of topics (and dumping the difficult tasks on absent members).

After the group discussions, the class is eager to get on with the research. Our next two classes are in the library. The first is conducted by a reference librarian, who is prepared to discuss approaches to the specific tasks at hand. Students are attentive during this library session—which could be dry and tedious—because of their particular interest. "How do I find out who the jurors were for the Scopes trial?" asks a student who has gotten started and run into trouble. The librarian emphasizes the differences in the strategies that must be used in researching events that happened in the recent past and ones that happened two centuries ago.

The following class period, we meet again in the library, this time to collect material. I drift while students sleuth. We have spoken in the classroom about the group nature of this task. "If you find material that will be useful to another member of your group, you must let him or her know." I emphasize the *total* presentation, not competition with the other group. It's important to help members of the other group, too: "Tina, show Joel how to use the microfilm." A cooperative spirit will make both presentations more interesting—and enhance the reading of the plays.

I try to make sure that each student is well started by the end of this period. There is only the rest of the week to finish the research.

On the dreaded report days, the actual reports proceed smoothly. As student after student contributes, the effect is cumulative. Group members break in spontaneously: "I found something else about that." "Oh, you explained something that I couldn't find." These class periods end on a high.

When we can find time, we review the process: "What difficulties did you have with your research?" "What worked well?" These discoveries are shelved, to be reexamined before the final term paper five weeks hence.

Meanwhile, we have the plays to read and comparative papers to write.

"Act I of *Inherit the Wind* for next class," I say, trying to get the groups to break up so that a waiting class can come into the room.

Julia walks by me, her face flushed, her eyes bright. Our eyes meet. We smile. I decide not to say anything.

9 Talking about Books: Readers Need Readers

Adele Fiderer
Scarsdale Public Schools
Scarsdale, New York

Lucy Calkins (1986) tells us that the books she remembers are those she has talked about. Alan Purves has said that it takes two to read a book. And Eileen, one of my fifth-grade students, writes, "Doing a book report alone after reading is boring. Getting to write questions and conferencing about a book is a heck of a lot more interesting 'cause you can do it with another person."

The book conferences that Eileen mentions take place in my fifth-grade classroom after two or more students have read the same book. My students, like those described by Nancie Atwell (1984), choose their own books, read them in class, write about their reactions to the books, and then confer with me and with their peers.

In my classroom it is the conference, the collaborative talk about books, that provides to readers the main mode of response and helps them become active, critical readers. Through talk readers discover what it is they really think about a book. Christenbury and Kelly (1983) tell us that "talking—asking and answering questions—often reveals our thoughts and feelings to us as well as to others" (p. 1). They point out that many of us don't really know what we think about an issue until we hear ourselves talking about the issue.

Xin-hua, another of my students, finds that collaborative talk does more than help her know what she thinks. The ideas offered by other readers expand her own vision. She writes, "When you talk about a book with someone who has read it, you and the person give your opinions about it. . . . When you disagree, you look at the book in a whole new way."

Preparing for the Collaboration

Questions and topics formulated in advance by students provide the structure for the book conferences. Although the readers may leave the question structure at any time during the conference, they are guided into purposeful talk by the questions or topics they have selected.

The following scenario illustrates what I do to help readers write questions that will encourage other students to respond from a variety of perspectives: literal recall of the text, personal interpretations and reactions to the text, and relevant personal experiences. Dominique was the first one in the class to complete *Do Bananas Chew Gum?*, by Jamie Gilson. She wrote the following questions to ask future readers of that book:

> Does Sam learn to read?
>
> Do Sam's classmates stop calling him "Cutes"?
>
> Did Sam decide to take the tests?
>
> What did Sam, Alex, and Chuck find in the tree?
>
> Did Wally find his retainer?
>
> Does Sam like Alicia?
>
> Why did people hate Alicia?

Since this was Dominique's first experience with question writing early in the school year, she met with me for a "rehearsal" conference to find out whether her questions would encourage someone to "talk a lot." She discovered that all of the questions except the last one elicited "yes," "no," or a single-word response.

Together we looked at a sample list of talk-provoking questions I had prepared. They began with phrases such as "Why did . . . ," "Why do you think . . . ," "What would you . . . ," "What if . . ." Some ended with "piggyback" questions such as "Why or why not?" and "What makes you think that?"

Then Dominique thought of ways she could revise her questions to help someone make full and interesting responses. Later, during the sharing time that concluded our reading workshop, Dominique heard other students tell about questions that promoted interesting discussions in their book conferences. Xin-hua had asked the following: "Would this book make it as a play? How could it be done and what part would you want?" and "On a scale of one to ten, what would you rate this book and why?"

Here are Dominique's revised questions:

> I wonder if Sam ever learned how to read. <u>How could he learn?</u>

I wonder why Sam had a reading problem. What do you think?

Why did people hate Alicia?

I wonder why they called the book *Do Bananas Chew Gum?*

What would you have called the book? Why?

Do you think Alicia gets braces? Would you want braces?

Do you think Sam has other friends besides Alicia and Wally? Who?

I wonder if Sam ever gets fired from baby-sitting? Do you?

Would you fire him? Why or why not?

After carefully recopying the revised questions onto a 9″ × 12″ prelined oak-tag card, Dominique printed the title and the date next to her name on a wall chart. This would let future readers of *Do Bananas Chew Gum?* know that she had prepared questions for a conference. Dominique then filed the card in a box and hoped she wouldn't have to wait long for another reader.

Dominique's chances of finding another reader for her book were good for two reasons. First, I had ordered multiple copies of good paperback books for our classroom library. (Students can choose books from home, community, school, or classroom libraries.) Second, in the book-sharing time that concludes each reading workshop, Dominique tried to attract another reader with a one-minute sales talk similar to the book commercial Jim Trelease recommends in *The Read-Aloud Handbook* (1982).

Maura thought that Dominique's book about a sixth-grade boy with both learning problems and girl problems sounded interesting, and she asked to read it next. Finally the stage was set for the collaboration.

The Book Conference

When Maura completed the book, she and Dominique sat together at a table in the corner of the room with the questions Dominique had written. Because it's important that the topics for the conference be meaningful to both participants, Maura selected the four questions that most interested her from the seven Dominique had written on the card. Then, on the back of the card, Maura wrote three topics or issues she wanted to discuss with Dominique.

To avoid a test-like tone and to encourage a dialogue, I ask both readers to respond to each question or topic that they've selected. As the two readers talk, I note collaborative behaviors and the learning that results. (If I cannot be present at a conference, I ask the students to tape-record their conversations.)

> *Dominique:* Why do you think that Sam didn't learn to read?
>
> *Maura:* I thought he was traveling around so much with his father that he didn't really have a chance to learn how to read. But he was a whiz in math, so he caught on easily to that, but he really didn't catch on easily with reading.
>
> *Dominique:* I think . . . Me and Mrs. Fiderer were talking about that, and some kids have dyslexia and spell backwards. He might have spelled pot as t-o-p.

In this portion of their talk each student presents her own interpretation of Sam's problem. Maura has made a good guess, and Dominique adds information from an outside source (my written response to something Dominique had written in her lecture log) that extends Maura's awareness of the main character's problem.

> *Dominique:* Why do some people hate Alicia?
>
> *Maura:* Because she was always showing off her grades, feeling that she was the best at everything . . .
>
> *Dominique:* Yeah.
>
> *Maura:* . . . that she knew everything and she used big words.
>
> *Dominique:* Yeah, I thought so, too. She thought she was so smart.

In the excerpt above, Dominique and Maura agree in their interpretation of a character. "Yeah" is the word students use most to show agreement and encouragement. Dominique interrupts Maura in mid-sentence with an encouraging "Yeah." They alternately contribute ideas and together build a larger portrait of Alicia than either would have constructed alone.

> *Dominique:* Do you think Sam will have other friends besides Wally and Alicia?
>
> *Maura:* Well, not yet, but I think he will get some when they find out that he's nice or not. He's alone because they think that he's dumb, but he's not.
>
> *Dominique:* You know, there's Chuck and Alex.
>
> *Maura:* He'll probably get new friends.

Now, stimulated by Dominique's question, the readers are conjecturing. Alan Purves (1968) cites such guessing about the future beyond the text as indicative of a reader's engagement and involvement with a book. In this case Dominique and Maura each predict a different "ending."

> *Dominique:* I wonder if Chuck gets fired from babysitting. Would you fire him?
>
> *Maura:* [Pause] No.
>
> *Dominique:* Why?
>
> *Maura:* Uh, [pause] because he had treasure hunts and he did things with them. And it was fun, I guess.
>
> *Dominique:* I thought I'd be a little sore at him because the kids should have gone with him. Like . . . you know . . . they should've gone with him instead of staying by themselves. So I'd be sore at him for a while.

Dominique's question "Would you fire him?" elicits "I'd be sore at him," a response that Purves would see as another example of a reader's engagement or involvement with the text. The readers here, like the mature readers studied by Purves, are reacting to "the world of the work as if that world were not fictional" (1968, p. 12).

This portion of the conference also illustrates some of the language patterns that occur in kids' talk about books. Their talk is natural—it has the sound and tempo of real speech. They pause, repeat themselves, and pepper their speech with "uh," "you know," and "like."

They also use a kid-to-kid language—speaking in their own vernacular to interpret characters and actions. Here Dominique uses one of her natural expressions, "sore at him," to indicate annoyance or anger. In another book conference Christina called Fudge, the young brother in *Tales of a Fourth Grade Nothing*, "a pain-in-the-butt." John described a character in *The Black Cauldron* as "a sloppy old jerk."

The conference continued:

> *Maura:* I'd like to talk about the spelling bee.
>
> *Dominique:* Yeah.
>
> *Maura:* And so I think that was funny when Alicia couldn't do it [i.e., spell *malocclusion*].
>
> *Dominique:* Yeah, I know, it was funny. [Their talk runs together and they laugh.] It was Friday the thirteenth, and I guess she had bad luck.
>
> *Maura:* It was Friday the thirteenth?
>
> *Dominique:* Yeah, remember?
>
> *Maura:* Oh, that's right. That was funny. What did Sam give her to spell?

Dominique: Molar [malocclusion] or something.

Maura: Alicia was giving people all hard words [Alicia and Sam were captains of the team for the spelling bee], and he gave her one she couldn't spell.

Dominique: Well, she forgot one letter. Friday the thirteenth must have given her bad luck.

Maura: Then she gave him "cute" and he couldn't spell it. He couldn't spell it because he had a reading problem and . . .

Dominique: [Interrupting] And everybody started calling him "Cutes" because he couldn't spell that.

In the talk above, Dominique nudges Maura's memory, attempting to supply her with facts that Maura forgot. My students do this regularly for each other in book talks, just as my friends and I do when we try to recall the details of a book we've shared. Laughter is frequent, too.

Not every question leads to involved discussion, I discovered. It's easy to recognize the perfunctory responses: talk doesn't bounce back and forth, nor do the readers leave the questioning structure. On the other hand, when the topic means something to one of the readers (usually the one who introduces it), the talk sparks. Each reader rushes to say something, and often one completes a sentence the other has begun. This kind of talk has the sound of passion.

For an example of this talk, we leave Dominique and Maura for a moment to join Danny and Michael, who are discussing *Taran Wanderer,* by Lloyd Alexander. Danny has asked Michael to describe three important people that Taran met in The Land of the Free Commots. This is a fairly literal recall question, and it doesn't produce much of a discussion. But when Danny asks how these people changed Taran's life, he fires up his own thinking. Michael, carried along by Danny's excitement, becomes a one-man cheering squad.

Danny: How did these people change Taran's life?

Michael: They helped him to learn things that would help him in his life—how to provide for himself. The Potter—uh—the Claymaker told him—gave him a lesson that some things, you know, are gifts, and some things, you just can't—uh, you just don't have it.

Danny: Like the Swordsmith—he taught him a lesson like—remember—it took him day after day to make a sword, and once he made a beautiful sword . . .

Michael: [Interrupting] Yeah!

Danny: . . . he swung it against the tree and it broke . . .

Michael: [Interrupting] Yeah!

Danny: . . . until it came out strong . . .

Michael: In a way he's saying that . . .

Danny: [Interrupting] . . . the way you look does not have anything to do with the way you are inside.

Michael: That's one of the lessons the Swordsmith told him.

Danny: The Weaver told him that every strand you weave is like a person's life . . .

Michael: Yeah!

Danny: . . . and if you let the string dangle, that would be your life.

Michael: Yeah, the Claymaker taught him that a gift you can't make; it's born with you.

Meanwhile, their conference over, Maura and Dominique walk together to a large chart titled "Readers Discuss Books." In one of the blank spaces next to Maura's name Dominique pencils in the book title, her own initials, and the date. They replace the question card in the file box, where it will await the next reader of their book.

Dominique and Maura have helped each other comprehend, analyze, and enjoy a book. Neither could have done it alone. It takes two to read a book.

References

Alexander, L. 1969. *The Black Cauldron.* New York: Dell.

———. 1969. *Taran Wanderer.* New York: Holt, Rinehart and Winston.

Atwell, N. 1984. Writing and Reading Literature from the Inside Out. *Language Arts* 61: 240–52.

Blume, J. 1986. *Tales of a Fourth Grade Nothing.* New York: Dell.

Calkins, L. M. 1986. *The Art of Teaching Writing.* Portsmouth, N.H.: Heinemann.

Christenbury, L., and P. P. Kelly. 1983. *Questioning: A Path to Critical Thinking.* Urbana, Ill.: National Council of Teachers of English.

Gilson, J. 1980. *Do Bananas Chew Gum?* New York: Lothrop, Lee & Shepard Books.

Purves, A. C., with V. Rippere. 1968. *Elements of Writing about a Literary Work.* Urbana, Ill.: National Council of Teachers of English.

Trelease, J. 1982. *The Read-Aloud Handbook.* New York: Penguin Press.

10 Group Presentations of Poetry

Muriel Ridland
University of California, Santa Barbara

Whatever our view of the theory of collaborative learning, those of us who have used group methods to further our teaching of composition or of understanding of a text know the value of small-group editing and discussion for increasing student competence and for developing more independent working habits. My most successful and significant use of student groups has been achieved through putting the students in charge of the class—not merely working together but actually becoming teachers. In my freshman English classes, it is common for students to present scenes from plays in the freshman English program; less common is the presentation of poems by one or two students (except occasionally in more advanced classes). Using the latter technique, I have successfully given over the class to my students through a series of group presentations of poetry that fulfill several objectives in the freshman curriculum.

In the second course of the required freshman composition and literature sequence, the subject matter for the ten-week quarter is equally divided between poetry and drama. I teach poetry first, and I have found that Robert Frost's *North of Boston* admirably serves as a bridge to Shakespeare's poetic drama (a course requirement). Frost's poems are fairly long; they are conceived dramatically, mostly in dialogue with occasional narrative comments; and they offer, in spite of their difficulty, some immediately accessible and comprehensible human situations that students can understand and yet be extended by. Frost's compassionate perceptions of misunderstanding and conflict between men and women and between different social classes are as thought-provoking as any contemporary material on sexual and societal roles. And the puzzles created by the tautness of the dialogue stimulate student discussion and group study. The poems also provide a perfect vehicle for group presentation.

Group Presentation Structure

I set up the poetry discussion and study as follows: each group will have one poem to work with. As far as possible, students are assigned to groups according to the number of voices in the poem. (Occasionally, in a monologue or lopsided dialogue, students share one part.) I choose the group members myself to try to balance skills the students have already demonstrated in reading aloud, responding in class discussion, and catching on to poems with more subtle personality factors that might affect group action. For example, two shy people may work well together if they are intelligent and capable, and they may help each other more than a timid person paired with a brash and dominating one. However, since the class has been meeting for only two weeks when I make the assignment, a good deal must be left to chance, and as always, chance works both for and against the project in about equal proportions.

I ask the students to read ahead and to indicate their preferences among the poems, but often they forget or their choices seem inappropriate, so I temper their preferences with my judgment of their abilities. Some students are angry at my choices, but anger has its uses: it is a strong response—infinitely more useful than indifference—and it usually leads to equally strong discoveries of interest and enjoyment. I do not assign the parts. I leave this up to the group, since the negotiating that takes place between students who want to read an unsuitable part and those who have more sense of the whole is part of the learning.

The students are provided with general instruction sheets that outline the task, including some quotations from Frost on poetry, brief explanatory comments on the book and its setting, and some general suggestions about understanding the assigned poem, preparing a class presentation, and developing questions to lead discussion. I warn the students of some of the problems with previous class presentations, and I emphasize the need for group preparedness. Even so, there seems always to be one group, especially at the beginning, that fails to meet beforehand. The resulting confusion is obvious to all, and such groups learn a humbling lesson about taking an assignment and its instructions seriously.

The students also know that their longest paper of the quarter and probably of the year (six to eight pages) will be an individual account of the process they went through in fulfilling this assignment. Giving instructions from the beginning about the writing assignment helps to ensure that students carry out the required preparation.

Further help consists of detailed sets of study questions on the individual poems, which draw attention to clues the students might overlook and to parts that are difficult. These questions may range from specifics such as "What sort of person is each speaker?" and "What do the first fifteen lines of 'One Hundred Collars' tell us about Dr. Magoon?" to more general questions such as "What seems to interest Frost most in this poem?" These questions are not intended to be used in class, though sometimes if the group is having difficulty entering into discussion they may fall back on them.

I also offer to meet with each group in my office for help with the poem. Weaker groups often need this assistance. However, the disadvantage of such assistance is that it removes the elements of surprise and independence—surprise for me during the class performance, and independent (even if sometimes muddled) understanding of the poem for the group.

Finally, I direct the first class meeting on *North of Boston* to provide a partial model for the groups' presentations. We listen to a tape of Frost reading "The Death of the Hired Man," and I lead the ensuing discussion, having previously provided study questions. Otherwise the task is up to the students.

After each presentation I ask the class to complete evaluation sheets. The questions on the sheet aim at producing discursive answers that judge the quality of the reading performance, its ability to convey tone and meaning, and the success of the discussion. These questions are answered anonymously by the audience and then given to the performers, who later return them to me (an ID number allows me to check which audience members have completed the evaluations and how much effort they have made). In addition, each audience member is asked how much work he or she put into preparing for the poem before the class presentation. The answers are remarkably candid. The necessity of judging the presentation keeps indifferent students alert, whereas the interested students are eager to comment on the reading and the discussion.

The Teacher's Role

What is the teacher's role in this process? I reserve the right to enter the discussion if it is weak, lagging, or wildly off course. I try to play devil's advocate, asking questions rather than taking over the discussion. But I must play my part with care. If I sit on the side of the room, all heads turn toward me when I speak (one inherits the authoritarian mantle of the teacher willy-nilly!). If I sit in the back, I divert less attention. Obviously, for the exercise to succeed, the less I speak, the better; yet some of the most lively meetings have resulted from some group's bizarre readings that are argued fiercely by the class only when I have roused the courage of a few doubters of the misreadings. For example, one group illustrated the power of a strongly expressed opinion to sway a whole class into ignoring evidence by enthusiastically interpreting the congenial-though-rough-necked traveling salesman in Frost's "One Hundred Collars" as a thief. There were only two dissenters, both too timid to push their view without my backing. This session was extremely enlightening for us all: I suggested that similar suppression by an authoritative group must often occur on juries, as well as in many areas of policy in politics and business.

In a more positive way, one of my most successful uses of this exercise resulted from the active responses of a very intelligent, feisty student who sat in the front row and attacked misreadings brilliantly about midway through each discussion. Students noted in their papers that they prepared themselves for her and that she kept them on their toes.

The Values of Group Presentation

What are the values promoted by these presentations? First, the class always discusses more freely than when the teacher is in charge. Students who will not speak, however gently I encourage them, become bold and argumentative when their fellow students propose an interpretation. All members of the performing group are forced to take part, and some develop surprising pugnacity in defending their group and individual views.

Second, having to practice reading the poem aloud develops both an awareness of words and rhythm and an awareness of meaning, as the following paragraph from a student account shows:

> Each time Samantha and I practiced the poem, we discovered something new about it. We learned how to emphasize key words, or perhaps put more emotion into certain lines or sections. The physical actions of the characters became more apparent, and I personally felt that I was *becoming* my character to some extent.

Such involvement leads to performances with dramatic and emotional power.

The autonomy of the group in choosing the parts and the methods of presentation also forces the students through some delicate negotiations. The following are two examples:

> When Tom and I talked about "The Code," I did not particularly agree with everything he said, but we really helped each other in understanding the individual lines. Even when we disagreed on the meaning of a passage, hearing someone else's point of view helped me form my own opinion.

> Throughout this experience, whether I was performing or a member of the audience, I think the key was that I was testing my ideas against those of my fellow students. Sometimes it is too easy to accept the opinions of your professors because of their experience and imposing demeanor, but with other students you feel you are on equal ground. By this interaction I was forced to scrutinize my own conclusions and rethink many of my first impressions.

In addition, a strong sense of shared purpose develops from working (and arguing) together, which carries the group through the nervousness—indeed in some cases terror—of performing in public. Some students have a crippling inability to speak in front of other people:

> When I first learned that we were going to have to perform a poem for the class, I was terrified. Reading aloud was such a severe problem that I repeated second grade. At UCSB I have been faced with many situations where it was more comfortable to be silent than to answer. . . . We first decided who was to read which part, and I wanted the easiest one. . . . I explained to my partners that I did not read well, but to my amazement found they were not much better at it than I. Somehow the uncomfortable knot in my stomach began to disappear and I ended up taking on the parts of two different characters. . . . It is still difficult to believe that after this one assignment at the age of twenty, I am now able to pick up any printed material and read it aloud with a fair amount of ease. It has been a major breakthrough for me to overcome a long-lasting mental block.

The liveliness and variety in the class sessions keep the students eager and intense. And along with having to state on the evaluation sheet how much work they put into preparing to listen to a poem, they are motivated by a desire not to let each other down—since a listless, unprepared class makes a nightmare of the discussion for the presenting group. ("The class at this point in the discussion had attained total brain death," a rueful student complained of a Monday class during midterms.)

One other advantage comes from the additional requirement to write a substantial paper on the group presentation and the poem itself. In the first half of this paper the students describe how they prepared for the presentation, which allows for inventiveness in selection of narrative detail, humor, and—among the more skilled—an intermixing of analysis of both the process and the poem's content. This narrative can include a progressive understanding of parts of the poem, as the writer describes the discussion among the group members about the characters and the plot.

By the time the students move to the second half of the paper, a discussion of the poem itself, they can transfer their confidence in writing about a personal experience to writing more analytically. Now their ability to find the most significant and interesting parts of the poem competes with the need to give some sense of the whole. They must select rigorously because by now they have enormous amounts of material and a mere summary will not be sufficient: the length of the poem and the openness of the topic create an organizational challenge that prevents boredom with familiar material.

These papers are invariably more interesting to read and more competently written than short papers written earlier in the term, where the task was elucidation of a poem concentrating on some element such as metaphor, imagery, or tone. From their experience in a group of peers, and as class discussion leaders, the students know their audience; the teacher has been only one member of a class that has already largely shared and approved their ideas. The students now have confidence from having succeeded in a difficult task, and the papers that follow are invariably more competent.

Advantages of the Collaboration Process

How much have the students learned about reading a poem? Certainly they have come up with less comprehensive detail about the poem itself than would emerge in a class discussion that I direct, since my individual experience in reading poems is probably much greater than all of theirs combined. However, what they have learned from their discussions will stick. The knowledge is their own, and the vast majority of students speak proudly in their papers of "our" or "my" poem. The weaker students, especially, describe the level of understanding they have reached as much greater than that from ordinary class discussion. While the teacher may raise more issues and seek a more elaborate reading through class discussion, I suspect that far less is absorbed or retained than what the students gain from their shared inquiry. As Kraft (1985) notes, "Students learn most permanently and with most pleasure in concert with other students. . . . [and] in an atmosphere of high feeling: enthusiasm, joy, even anger" (p. 152). There is a delight expressed by so many students about understanding "their" poem, and a sense of accomplishment that is only partly equaled later in the term by successful performances of scenes from Shakespeare (for that requires acting skills of a different order, which many students do not possess). "I did it myself"is the underlying message of their papers, and that is clearly accurate, even though the individual success results from collaboration. In the end, I am sure they remember and understand far more than they do when I purvey "information" during discussion.

Another advantage of the collaborative learning assignment comes from the requirement to complete a series of steps, concluding with a written report that has been seen as an end from the very beginning. The work is carried out to completion over several weeks, is divided into clearly delineated stages, and contains within it a condensed experience of all the objectives of the course: to learn more about how to read poetry, to become conscious of the sound of poetry by reading it aloud, to discover some of the principles of dramatic structure, and to experience the force of dramatic dialogue. Further, my students learn that all inquiry depends on cooperation with others—building upon their ideas through a collaborative process—and, very significantly, that the best way to conclude a train of thought is with a measured piece of writing.

The dangers that may underlie the theory and practice of collaborative learning rest in emphasizing consensus, which, as Kenneth Bruffee (1984) acknowledges, may result in "conformity, anti-intellectualism, intimidation, and leveling-down of quality" (p. 652). Group judgment may overwhelm the truly brilliant innovator, the one who has the potential to emerge from the group and become one of the few who will influence and change not just the group's thinking but potentially the thinking of the "interpretive community" or even that of the larger society. Do such minds dominate the group and thus nullify the concept of collaboration, or are they instead crushed by the process of "intellectual negotiation"? I believe that the multifaceted nature of the group task I set allows for, and even encourages, individual brilliance as well as the generative effects of group negotiation and cooperation. The individual performances and papers vary greatly in quality, with some readers showing exquisite awareness of every nuance of language and feeling—making clear that their grasp of the material operates at a very different level from that of their peers. Thus the whole experience generates the possibility of truly imaginative effort rather than a stifling of imagination.

Any collaborative learning activity makes possible many of the advantages listed above. I believe that my classes advance the process one step further when the students take charge of the classroom. Having to lead discussion forces them to take responsibility for what they think and say. It gives them invaluable experience in speaking out in front of a highly critical (though basically sympathetic) audience. The whole process etches into their minds the value of collaboration and the subtle interchanges of negotiation—not only on a personal level but as a means for establishing competence in the study of literature and for becoming novice members of an academic group or "discourse community." The experience also illustrates to them the advantages of taking risks, standing up for what they believe, reassessing strong opinions in the light of new evidence (which doesn't always happen in general discussion), and taking responsibility for their own learning. Above all, as the director of the South Coast Writing Project*, Sheridan Blau, has suggested to me, they discover that their own behavior helps determine the quality of their classroom instruction. They now understand that the teacher is dependent on the students' responses. The collaborative work of the small group is thus an excellent model for the intellectual proceedings in the class—and, potentially, in the university as a whole.

References

Bruffee, K. A. 1984. Collaborative Learning and the "Conversation of Mankind." *College English* 46: 635–52.

Frost, R. 1983. *North of Boston, Poems*. Dodd, Mead.

Kraft, R. G. 1985. Group Inquiry Turns Passive Students Active. *College Teaching* 33, no. 4: 149–54.

*A site of the National Writing Project located at the University of California, Santa Barbara.

III Collaboration in Writing, Revising, and Editing

ploy collaborative strategies in teaching reading and writing to initiate students into the "conversation of mankind." And there is evidence that these strategies are increasingly being implemented in writing instruction. For at least the last ten years, the use of writing groups in the classroom has been promoted (Graves 1983; Hawkins 1976; Healy 1980). Teachers have been urged to turn their classrooms into communities of writers. Response groups suggest to student writers ways of improving their papers. Student editors work with their peers on revision and proofreading. At the many sites of the National Writing Project, teachers also are sharing their writing with others in small groups. These strategies seem to be working very successfully. They foster the idea that writing deserves to be taken seriously, and they help even very young children participate in the "conversation of mankind."

In spite of the increasingly collaborative pedagogy and the focus on writing as a process, however, the end product desired is still overwhelmingly the individually authored piece of writing. Gebhardt noted in 1980 that most classroom groups are used to respond to drafts already written by individuals, and although he urges broadening the base of collaboration in writing, I have seen since then very little evidence that collaboration regularly embraces more than the proofreading and editing stages. The very names *editing group* and *response group* suggest their limited function. Adams and Thornton report that the reason most academic writers undertake to collaborate is that their projects are "too large to complete alone" (p. 25). Since many students regard *any* writing task as too large to complete alone, perhaps even too large to *start* alone, it seems reasonable to allow them to take advantage of the kind of help that professional writers are not ashamed to seek—collaboration.

It may be difficult to move away from the notion of individual composing as the ideal. (Adams and Thornton report that even the collaborators they interviewed still believed in it). One reason is probably that our pedagogy has emphasized the individual theme, individual correction by a teacher, and individual conferences. But there is no reason to apologize for collaboration; it is not necessary to write in a vacuum. If teachers believe that their students can benefit from imitating the practices of scientists, scholars, journalists, and business people, there are ways in which they can deliberately promote collaborative writing at all stages of the process. The following are some specific suggestions, each of which has its counterpart in the "real world."

The Invention Stage

1. Two or more persons discuss an idea and its possible development; one person does the actual writing. William Wordsworth's works owe much to his constant companionship and conversation with his sister, Dorothy (Manley 1974). John Stuart Mill's wife, Harriet, collaborated with him even more closely, sharing discussion of the actual language as well as the ideas in his works (Mill 1961). Many authors acknowledge in the dedications of their books similar contributions from spouses, colleagues, or friends. On a more mundane level, this sort of collaboration is frequently practiced by committees, where one person is delegated to write up the consensus reached by the group.

Even in classrooms in which individual writing is expected, students can profit from collaboration during the invention stage of the writing process. They can help each other avoid the writing vacuum by discussing ideas, approaches, and details. Such discussions, in addition to aiding writing, also provide excellent practice in speaking and listening skills.

2. Several writers pool notes they have collected and share them. This strategy is especially useful for projects involving the gathering of data. Students may amass more material than they can use or material only tangentially related to their narrowed topic. Spiegelhalder describes the "lively interchange of notecards and xerox copies" (p. 100) that occurs in his class when students are deciding on their final arrangement for the group paper. At the university level, colleagues often share articles they come upon that pertain to each other's research interest. There is no reason that student colleagues shouldn't do the same.

A variation of this note-sharing technique that could easily be adapted for a class assignment was reported to me by two colleagues, both of whom attended a school board meeting to hear a debate on an issue of professional concern to them. Both took notes for the report they were to write, but instead of writing from their own notes, they exchanged and each wrote from the other's. They found it uncomfortable to do so, yet each felt that it helped him to see things from a different perspective and to include points that he might otherwise have missed. One can hardly insist on the truth being what he or she has witnessed if it is contradicted by what someone else has also witnessed. Like historians and journalists, my colleagues had the task of trying to distill from their different accounts the truth of what "really happened."

then writes an article reporting the results, incorporating whatever sentences or phrases from the letters that are the most quotable. The compilers of reports from questionnaires follow much the same procedure. A class might create a composite essay or letter to the editor this way, with several of the strongest writers doing the shaping. Since almost every paper is likely to have at least one good example or striking phrase, the finished work will include more detail and more vivid and effective language than any one person is likely to produce.

The Revision Stage

1. One person puts together the chunks written by several others, often including his or her own chunk. This is what Thomas Jefferson did for the framers of the Constitution, what editors of collections do, and what committee secretaries do. My students would have done better to designate one of their group to provide this service. In a class situation, it might be fairer to have one member of a group, instead of writing a chunk, be the Thomas Jefferson who puts it all together.

2. One person revises, enlarges, and updates the work of an earlier writer. The classic example of this model is E. B. White's expansion of William Strunk's "little book," written many years earlier, to produce Strunk and White's *The Elements of Style.* Some older works can be revised for fun and exercise. A few years ago, one of my students brought to class a little pamphlet written in the fifties containing tips on dating, dressing, and other matters of social etiquette. While certain examples were dated, much of the advice was still sound, and the whole thing could profitably have been revised for today's teens. Works need not be thirty-five years old, however; certain works such as school histories and student handbooks regularly need updating.

Another variation is to have students revise a piece of writing for a different audience. For example, they might adapt directions for an experiment from a high school chemistry manual to a sixth-grade reading level. Proficient writers could provide a real service by revising text materials for classmates who are ESL students.

3. One person reorganizes and edits a draft written by someone else. Although some editors return to contributors any manuscripts that need major revisions, others (and I am one) make revisions themselves. The usual practice of editing groups is to point out problems and make suggestions for improvement, then return the work to the original writer to revise. Romantic individualism again! It would be equally possible for one student to take another's draft and revise it. Students could also be asked to look for examples of badly written published prose to revise. Often a letter to the editor will have a valid point to make but make it so badly that I, for one, always have an urge to rewrite it. Another source is fourth-class mail, in which appeals from various political and charitable groups predominate. These appeals are usually overmodified, repetitive, and replete with logical fallacies—in short, ripe for rewriting. Such materials are to be found everywhere.

As I hope these examples have shown, collaborative writing is a pedagogical strategy that deserves to be tried. It can help reduce student anxiety and build group rapport through shared responsibility. The discussion and interaction that take place at every stage can promote learning and retention by bringing the writing process to conscious awareness. And the unity and style of students' written products are likely to be better than most could produce on their own. We do students a disservice when we insist that they spin everything out of their own guts, telling them they will always have to do so in the world outside the classroom. Like so many educational myths, this one crumbles in the cold air of reality. Writing doesn't occur in a vacuum; writers don't have to begin with a blank page.

Bibliography

Adams, P. G., and E. S. Thornton. 1986. An Inquiry into the Process of Collaboration. *Language Arts Journal of Michigan* 2 (Spring): 25–28.

Bruffee, K. A. 1984. Collaborative Learning and the "Conversation of Mankind." *College English* 46: 635–52.

Ede, L., and A. Lunsford. 1983. Why Write . . . Together? *Rhetoric Review* 1 (January): 151–57.

———. 1985. Let them Write—Together. *English Quarterly* 18 (Winter): 119–27.

———. 1986. *Research on Co- and Group Authorship in the Professions: A Preliminary Report*. Paper presented at the annual convention of the Conference on College Composition and Communication.

Ferro, M. 1984. Presentation at annual Panal-Gila Conference on Teaching Writing, Central Arizona College, Coolidge, Arizona.

Gebhardt, R. 1980. Teamwork and Feedback: Broadening the Base of Collaborative Writing. *College English* 42: 69–74.

Graves, D. 1983. *Writing: Teachers and Children at Work*. Exeter, N.H.: Heinemann.

Hawkins, T. 1976. *Group Inquiry Techniques for Teaching Writing*. Urbana, Ill.: ERIC/RCS and NCTE.

process, they are encouraged to consult with classmates. Because each student works at a different pace, and because the groups are small, I have the students select who they want to work with at a given time. Writing with others became fun for the students as they discovered and exchanged new ideas, recognized old ones, weighed possibilities, and considered their own needs as readers.

Topic Selection

Topic selection is the first step in the writing process. At the beginning of a new cycle, when most of the students have completed their previous writing assignment, I present a new topic for writing.

The students also have individual topic lists that they develop during a class session. If a student chooses not to write on the topic I present, he or she can choose one from his or her own list. If still undecided on a topic, the student can choose one from a friend's list, or I will direct him or her to others whose lists offer interesting options.

This sharing works equally well when a student wants to add topics to his or her list; he or she simply goes around the room collecting ideas. Those still working on the previous assignment merely add my topic to their lists, and if they next choose to write on that topic, they will benefit by the experience of the speedier students working on the same topic, noting the directions they have taken and the options they have created.

When the semester first began, I presented topics designed to elicit personal responses ("New Year's Resolution," "About Myself," "Dreams," etc.). Later, I presented assignments directly related to units in science ("Universe," "Stars," "Constellations," etc.), social studies ("Chinese New Year's," "Myths"), and reading ("Fables," "Fairy Tales").

The following are sample topic lists, a third grader's and a fifth grader's. Whenever Danny, the fifth grader, completed his assignments, he worked with continuing interest on his list, which was entitled "Things I Like to Do" (here in its shortened form):

Danny's topic list	Bobby's Topiks
Going to Castle Park	my friend Steve
Going to the beach	my bad friend Andrew
Going surfing	my good friend
Playing sports	my enamea [enemy]

Riding my bike	my lion dance club
Reading my book	me and Roy
Computer games	
Watching t.v.	
Collecting keychains	
Going to the restaurant	

Though Bobby, the third grader, had a short topic list, he wrote stories about his lion dance club all semester long—and his stories grew fascinating. With my help, Bobby compiled them into a book at the end of the semester. The following are two of Bobby's stories, the first written at the beginning of the semester and the second toward the end.

MY NEW YEAR'S RESOLUTION
BY BOBBY

My New Year's resolution is not to be afraid of the lion dance because when I was a little boy I used to be afraid of the lion dance all the time.

But now I'm not afraid of the lion dance. Now I'm going to join only if I can do the lion dance. My mom let me join but I don't know if I can stay in because I'm not good at Kung Fu.

My lion dance master is thinking and he said to my mom, "I might really let Bobby stay in." The past few weeks he had been thinking about it. The End.

OUR LIONS' FUNERAL
BY BOBBY

On Sunday we went to Palolo's temple and we gave some food to the old lions before they go to bed for the last time. This is a ceremony where the master burns the lions because they are too old.

After they went to bed, we got the drums, the lion's head and the teasing mask. Then we started a fire and we burned the lion heads.

When the lion heads were burning, the eyeballs popped out. After they burned, the spirits came out. Each of the four lion heads had one eye missing.

That night the spirits came to my house with the drums. I saw them floating outside the window. It was so noisy I could not sleep. I saw the lions and it was fun. When the lions went home, I had good luck after all.

The next day, one of the lions that came at night dropped his tail in the yard and I now have the tail. The End.

punctuation is the last step. While a reader is editing, the writer sits next to him or her, answering questions, listening to ideas, and trying to understand why corrections are being made.

Because this was the students' first experience with process writing, I began their editing assignment by having them look for the writer's 5 W's & H (Who, What, When, Where, Why, and How). They were to apply these questions to any statement or fact that begged clarification. As a general guideline, the 5 W's & H helped the students edit for details and idea expansion.

When a student edits, he or she uses a colored pen to mark the manuscript, then signs his or her name at the bottom of the page. The second editor chooses a pen of a different color so the different markings can be distinguished.

I do the final editing with each student, explaining why I make certain corrections or asking them to clarify a sentence for me. In this way, they learn how to edit: what kind of things to look for, how to ask other students to explain what they wrote in order to make their sentences clearer, or how to edit other students' work without hurting their feelings.

In addition to receiving a grade for their final paper, each student receives a grade for the number of times they have edited and for the effectiveness of their editing.

Publishing

When most students are finished with their assignment, we have a Sharing Day. Everyone already feels a part of someone else's story because they have helped each other, and they share a feeling of anticipation and pride as the stories are read. During this sharing period, the students again make comments on their classmates' writings. These comments become more specific as the students sharpen their editing skills.

Sometimes students enjoy helping each other so much that they begin writing stories together. And another mode of writing emerges: students become coauthors, encouraging each other to complete their work and sparking each other's ambition. Also, much more discussion must take place because ideas need to be clear for both to write. I then see freewriting turning into complicated maps and outlines. The approach of two authors writing is also interesting. Some partners take turns writing paragraphs, while other partners work on separate chapters.

Writing together is fun. Students share ideas, help each other, and form new friendships, making for many writing and publishing possibilities: a class book, a published newsletter sent home to parents, a social studies report, or thank-you letters and other correspondence. These are all student ideas and choices, and this individual decision making is perhaps the seventh and final step in the writing process, resulting in empowered writers who are interested in nurturing their own growth.

fied as I learned more each year about the teaching of writing. But simply having something to begin with made it easier for me to believe (particularly on bad days, when there seemed to be nothing happening in an educational sense) that tomorrow would be better. I would search the list for some evidence of forward movement, and I would find *something* to maintain my faith. Venturing off the beaten path of inflexible lesson plans, teacher's guides, and large-group instruction was a frightening experience for a novice, and I needed constant reassurance.

The skills in which I wanted my students to demonstrate progress as they worked in classroom revision groups fell into three broad categories: (1) maintaining individual identity within the group, approaching the group with self-confidence, and establishing ownership of the written piece; (2) using the advice/suggestions of the group wisely to improve one's writing; and (3) developing the skills of group interaction (for example, helping and supporting fellow authors). In the list of skills, I identified, under each broad statement, specific student behaviors that would indicate to me that there was progress. The quotes within the following list were transcribed from tapes that were made while students participated in group revision.

I. Maintains identity within the group, approaches the group with self-confidence, and establishes ownership of his or her piece.

    A. Defends ideas and choice of development, such as action of character, against onslaught of options: "Some people do that." "He would say that."

    B. Screens responses of others. Decides which are significant: "I don't think it would sound right." "I tried that." "I can think about opinions and maybe use them. You have a choice to use the advice or not."

    C. Does not apologize before reading.

    D. Demands clarification of comments: "I don't know what you meant by that." "I don't understand."

    E. Assumes control of discussion by initiating suggestions for changes in his or her own piece. Recognizes and verbalizes his or her own perceived weaknesses before discussion. Examples: Recognizes when all is not related to the main idea; says, "I need to rephrase that." Or "hears" need for punctuation.

    F. Interchanges roles of creator and critic. Becomes a writer reading as a reader. Anticipates readers' questions.

G. Rejects or argues about suggestions, including ones offered by the teacher. (For example, I tried to give a teenaged character adult actions and motivations. The author pointed out my error.)
H. Selects among possibilities.
I. Modifies suggestions to create ownership.
J. Writes with a strong voice.

II. Uses advice/suggestions of the group wisely to improve writing. Learns from previous experience.
   A. Corrects/improves piece based on comments.
   B. Changes real event to improve narrative idea. Fictionalizes reality. Demonstrates flexibility.
   C. Appears open to comments. Sees that draft is not final.
   D. Develops respect for the reader, who is now seen as a significant other. Communication becomes important. Develops idea thoroughly by anticipating readers' questions.
   E. Brainstorms orally possibilities for alternatives/changes, then discusses logic of each.
   F. Breathes life into characters. Uses suggestion of need for dialogue. Lets characters speak for themselves.
   G. Bases idea for story on personal experience. Writes about what he or she knows. Narrows focus to a specific meaningful aspect of an experience.
   H. Experiments with a variety of genres and techniques. Succeeds in previously unsuccessful genre.
   I. Anticipates the ending in the beginning or middle using foreshadowing and/or well-planned plot development. Exhibits story cohesiveness.
   J. Attends to word choice to facilitate communication of precise meaning.

III. Develops skills of group interaction and helps/supports other authors.
   A. Responds to comments. Willing to be drawn out, stimulated by group.
   B. Perceives suggestions as support rather than criticism.
   C. Tries ideas out on group members: "I'm just talking . . ."
   D. Demands feedback. Recognizes when there's not enough. Elicits comments from group: "Should I put in . . . ?" "I need help with . . ." "I don't know how . . ." "That's hard! I don't know what I could put."
   E. Supports an author's defense.
   F. Demonstrates confidence in his or her role of group mem-

14 Building Effective Student Writing Groups

Jeffrey S. Copeland
University of Northern Iowa

Earl D. Lomax
David Lipscomb College

The students are in writing groups, five students per group. Today each student has a draft of a "personal narrative" for other members of the group to examine. The teacher says, "Be constructive today and be *specific* with your comments! Remember to use the comments of the other group members when you revise your drafts." The teacher then returns to a desk at the front of the room, and the students are told to begin. However, after five minutes the teacher glances up (distracted by the silence) to discover that the students in the writing groups are staring off into space or doodling on notebook paper.

Sound familiar? Most teachers who use student writing groups in the classroom will notice students reacting this way at one time or another. However, this scene doesn't have to be the norm when writing groups are at work in the classroom. Building effective writing groups involves much more than just herding students into groups of four or five and telling them to talk about a piece of writing. It requires a good deal of care and structuring. It is also a fairly time-consuming process, but once effective groups have been established, the benefits to the students are immense. Effective writing groups can be built by leading students through four natural developmental stages: apprehension, initial success, constructive criticism, and independence.

Stage I: Apprehension

Initially, for many students the idea of sharing a piece of writing with other members of a group ranks right up there with memoriz-

1. Have you experienced a similar event in your own life? Tell the others how it was similar.

2. Which section of the writing seemed most vivid or alive? What made it so?

3. What feelings did the characters in the writing show? How did this add to the writing?

4. As a reader, what were you thinking about at the end of the writing?

Note that these questions are designed to produce neutral or positive comments. The emphasis at this stage should be placed upon fostering discussion—not leading students to a critical explication of the work being examined. The initial response keys should also contain questions that require a personal response from the reader in order to let the writer know the effect the writing is having. These responses help build a foundation of trust and sharing within the groups, which in turn makes it easier for students to deal with constructive criticism.

Stage III: Constructive Criticism

Students soon begin to grope for something "more important" to discuss about the writing. This lets the teacher know that it is time to add constructive criticism to the process. If, however, the students have spent the last few writings giving nothing but neutral or positive comments and are suddenly told to shift to a more critical mode of response, the writing can suddenly become a jigsaw puzzle with several key pieces missing. The teacher can provide these missing pieces by helping the students create a more detailed response key for each assignment. These response keys should be tailored to reflect the aspects of the writing being specifically practiced and explored in the assignment. Thus, if the students are studying a new method of prewriting, the use of transitions, or whatever, the response key should direct them to discuss those areas. One pitfall here is limiting student discussion only to the areas mentioned in the response key. The key should not be the only source of discussion. On the contrary, students should be told that the questions will simply provide a place for discussion to begin and that they may also talk about any other areas they wish to examine (questions from earlier keys, material from class discussion, etc.). As the students move from assignment to assignment, the response keys will become less and less important. Eventually, the students gain enough practice through using the various response keys that they become good judges of what needs to be discussed in any given writing. Consciously or unconsciously, they develop a fairly detailed rubric to use when examining writing.

It should also be noted that it is quite common at this stage to find one or two students per group dominating the discussion. To make sure that all students have an opportunity for equal participation, and to make sure that the groups don't end up discussing *only* Aunt Anita or Uncle Joe in Nebraska, it helps to provide a few guidelines for functioning as a group. Sample guidelines can be found in Peter Elbow's (1973) *Writing without Teachers*. Elbow's suggestions include the following:

1. Never quarrel with someone else's reaction.
2. Be quiet and listen (directed to the writer).
3. Give specific reactions to specific parts.
4. Don't reject what readers tell you. (pp. 94–102)

This direction will help focus discussion and add to the positive climate being established within the groups.

Stage IV: Independence

This stage will often produce some surprises for the teacher. Even though the groups still need guidance and writing instruction from the teacher, many groups simply act as if they do not. After all, students reason, they are veterans now and mini-experts on the writing styles and writing flaws of their fellow group members. What else could they possibly need to know? Some groups become downright clannish and frown upon any interruption while they are working. (At the same time, it is also possible at this stage for some groups still to be groping along.)

At this stage, the teacher's role becomes that of a resource person for the groups and a "traveling writing expert." The teacher needs to move from group to group, answering questions and giving writing instruction as the students need it or ask for it. The end result is a delightful situation: students who through group work are now interested enough to ask about something in the writing can ask the willing and ready teacher for assistance. Ah, bliss!

Like anything practiced with regularity, the workshop process can become old hat to the group members. A little diversity thrown in

and sometimes I let them form their own groups. This part has never posed a problem, especially at the senior level.)

Once students are assembled, they discuss the thesis they wish to develop, the concession(s) they want to acknowledge, and the proofs upon which they wish to elaborate. Next, they assign themselves parts of the essay. For example, one person agrees to write the introduction and conclusion; another the concession paragraph, and the other three the support paragraphs.

For example, if the students are to write about the grading system, they first have to agree on a thesis. Assuming that their thesis favors the grading system, they next have to decide on concessions. They may want to concede the idea that giving letter grades encourages students to work "just" for the grade and not for knowledge. Next they decide on at least three supports for their thesis. The students may want to develop the importance of grades for college entrance, as rewards for hard work, or as gauges of self-progress. They also have to agree on the order in which to present their proof. The person who composes the introduction must complement the ideas presented in the body of the paper by composing a clearly defined thesis and suggesting the rationale that will be used to support it. This person must also present an appropriate summary statement. If the students do not finish their respective parts during the classroom period, they must do them as homework.

The next day the groups reconvene, and each student reads his or her part. (Group members should have a photocopy of each paragraph so that they can follow along as students read their paragraphs aloud.) They evaluate each other's work and rewrite their parts, adding transitions or making any other necessary changes. After finishing the revisions, students turn in the final product, which consists of several pages labeled "Introduction," "Concession Paragraph," "First Support Paragraph," "Second Support Paragraph," "Third Support Paragraph," and "Conclusion."

That evening, instead of having twenty-five or thirty papers from one class to check, I have only five or six and can spend more time evaluating. I do this by making taped critiques of the cooperative essays, being very specific about what is good or what can be improved in each paragraph. I pay attention to organization, development, logic, and style.

The next day, the students again gather in various corners of the classroom and listen to the taped critiques. (For this part of the lesson, I sign out five or six cassette players from the A-V department.) I practice what Carol Cummings calls "management by wandering around the classroom,"* and am available for further conferences if the taped critique needs clarification. Finally, I encourage the students to rewrite their particular parts of the essay if too many errors surface.

Since this activity is only practice for the real thing, I assign only five to ten points to each student for his or her part. The students appreciate the dry run. It gives them much more confidence for the next assignment, which they have to complete on their own and which is worth one hundred points.

Once I started assigning group essays, the individual essays improved considerably; student confidence increased, and the kids actually looked forward to writing. When I had them evaluate the class at the end of the year, they rated this activity as one of the most helpful.

I have shared this lesson plan with many of my colleagues who were also skeptical about "group tactics." Many of them have added their own personal touch to the technique, but all have found it a successful method that is beneficial to students and well worth the noise and dishevelled classrooms.

Reference

Baker, S. 1981. *The Practical Stylist.* 5th ed. New York: Harper and Row.

---

*ITIP Workshop, Troy School District, November 1986.

16 Ensuring the Success of Peer Revision Groups

Edgar H. Thompson
Neff Education Center
Emory, Virginia

Peer revision has long been advocated by writing teachers. However, many teachers I have talked to, particularly those at the upper middle-school and high school levels, have found that when they asked their students to work in small revision groups, the groups frequently degenerated into gossip sessions that focused on everything except the writing. I believe that all teachers can have successful peer revision groups in their classrooms if they will do three things with their students. First, students need to see a demonstration of how small revision groups operate; that is, what they can expect and what kinds of things should be happening if the group is functioning properly. Second, teachers need to carefully monitor students' progress as the students learn how to engage in this important collaboration. Finally, as the need arises, students may need to be given a refresher demonstration to illustrate how something has gone awry and why things aren't going as well as they should.

The Initial Demonstration

Of the three steps mentioned above, providing students with a clear demonstration of what should be happening in peer revision groups is the most complex. During my demonstration session, I use three sample student papers, two of which I will present here.* I tell students that these papers were actually written by college freshmen, though they weren't written by students in any of my classes. I pass

---

*The sample papers come from an inservice presentation I attended several years ago. The presenter at this meeting tells me that "What Cheerleading Means to Me" was written by one of his students a long time ago, while "An Embarrassing Experience" comes from a book or other source that he can no longer trace.

out the first paper, entitled "An Embarrassing Experience," to my students. I ask them to read it and then to write a response to the author on the back of the paper, as if they were a teacher responding to this author's work.

An Embarrassing Experience

When I were in high school we had a football Banquite and I had not Ben to a fromer accesson Befor. and I also included a young lady along.

I were like the young man in the story we read in class.

I came to the Banquite Poper dressed But I did not have no table Manner. Everyone Began to set down, I did not know I sirpose to assit the young lady with chair until she told me. after about 30 min they guss spoke Began to spake & I did not know when to Began to eat & after I saw all the other People eating I look around for my silverware, But I did not have any, then I tryed to get the water attanson. They finily Brage me my silverware. I thought that were the lose embarrassment monet for tonight, But they had just Began. The main dish were chicken & it were fried cripe & when I Bit off it, it would make a loud nose and the other People would look aroung at me & my date would look the other way. From then on I promer myself I would learn good table manner.

After students have had a few minutes to read this paper and write their responses, I ask them to share what they've written. Most students usually figuratively tear the paper to shreds, criticizing the inaccurate use of grammar, the poor spelling, and the incorrect punctuation. (Some student responses are more humane, especially when they have previously been exposed to the process approach to writing.) After several students read their reactions to the paper, I read mine, which usually goes something like this:

I know what it is like to be in such situations. I've been put in embarrassing situations many times in my life.

1. Why don't you write some more about what happened to you at the banquet?
   · Did people rib you later?
   · What did your girlfriend say to you?
2. Something else: Typically capital letters are needed only at the beginning of a sentence or with proper nouns (actual names of things, like Robert or St. Louis). Go back through your paper and add capital letters where you need them and remove them elsewhere.

When I ask students what the difference is between my response and theirs, they always recognize that I responded first to the content of the paper, specifying what I liked about it or what I empathized with. They also note that I made a comment aimed at helping the student to expand the content. In addition, they notice that I chose only one so-called mechanical issue, in this case a relatively simple one of capitalization. Through their observations and our further discussion, students come to recognize that attacking another student's writing or pointing out more errors than another student can handle only inhibits the process of working together to improve their writing. I emphasize that they do need to be honest, but there is no reason that they can't be honest in a caring, helpful fashion. I suggest they give feedback in much the same way they hope to receive it. Finally, I tell them it is best to identify something positive about the paper before moving on to items or issues that may need to be resolved during revision.

Ground Rules

At this point in the demonstration, I discuss some of the ground rules for working in small groups. I tell them that they must decide as individuals or as a group if they want their papers read silently or aloud. I don't care which option they choose. It's up to them to decide how they want to share their writing with other group members.

I recommend to them that reading their own paper out loud, or having someone else do so, is a useful strategy. At every stumbling point during the reading, they should make a notation in the text (or in a copy of text). The cause of the stumble may be a simple problem, such as poor handwriting, but there may also be a problem with the wording of the text or perhaps a left-out word. Whatever the cause, places where the reading doesn't progress smoothly should be carefully examined later. I also tell students that as their papers are read aloud, group members are forced to pay attention to the larger rhetorical issues in the paper. Since they don't have the actual text in front of them, the members can't be distracted by surface or proofreading issues. Also, while listening, group members have the freedom to write questions they have about the paper without interrupting the reading. These questions can be discussed later with the whole group and may lead to specific suggestions for revision.

I do tell students that they can have their papers read silently, but that this approach can be time-consuming and can weaken the quality of the feedback given. For example, if every student reads each other's paper in a round-robin manner, by the time all of the papers have been read, even if the size of a group is only three members, the immediacy of what each student remembers from the first paper may be lost. I recommend to them that if they want their papers to be read silently, they should bring at least two photocopies with them so that the papers can be dealt with one at a time.

Role Playing

After this brief discussion of options for sharing their papers, I ask three or four students whom I have talked to ahead of time (so they will be at ease) to come up to the front of the room and form a circle with their chairs. I tell the rest of the class to watch as we participate in a mock revision group. I play the role of the writer of the following paper, entitled "What Cheerleading Means to Me." I try to get into the role of the real author and read the essay as I think she would have read it.

What Cheerleading Means to Me

Ever since I can remember, I've always wanted to be a cheerleader. When I went to my first game, I was very impressed by the cheerleaders. They put spirit and excitement in the air, and made the crowd come alive.

In the spring of my seventh grade year I tried out. Luckily for me my best friends sister was a cheerleader. She took some time to help us learn the cheers and jumps that were required. I did not think I had a chance of making it. But my high hopes did not let me down. Making it was one of the happiest days of my life.

I believe cheerleading has helped me to become a more responsible and understanding person. I have been a cheerleader for the past five years, and was chosen varsity captain my senior year. Being chosen as captain was indeed the highest honor, I could have ever dreamed of and because I was the leader I tried my hardest to set the goal of perfection for myself, my squad, and my school.

One incident that happened my senior year, I believe shows how important cheerleaders are in promoting spirit for the athletic teams. Our football team had lost the past three games. Spirit and enthusiasm was at a very low level. Some of the students didn't even bother to attend the games. Seeing how low the moral of the school was becoming, the cheerleaders made posters advertising the games, sponsored pep rallies and dances. We tried to show the football team the whole school was behind them and knowing this, encouraged the team to try harder. Our season ended very successfully.

I have learned that cheerleading is so much more than just

wearing a uniform and screaming. I believe a cheerleader should have three important qualities: responsibility, leadership, and personality.

Of course, students enjoy my reading of the essay, since I don't look anything like a cheerleader, male or female. When I'm finished reading the essay, still in character, I ask the group what they think. They usually start by saying something positive, and then proceed to make some pertinent, useful comments. I resist everything they say, no matter how accurate. After I've done this for a minute or two, I ask the group members how they are feeling. They say they're about to give up because I won't listen to what they have to say. Their observations allow me to reinforce the importance of listening to what others say when receiving feedback. The students see that if they become defensive, the quality of the feedback will diminish. The tendency to become defensive is a common one for all of us. I tell them that when my wife reads something I've written, if I'm not careful, we get into a fight, which is really wasted effort. If I can keep my mouth shut and listen, however, in a short time I usually realize that what my wife is saying is right. Besides, no matter what I think, I have to respect what my audience, my readers, tell me. I encourage my students to do the same.

Before moving on to the next part of the demonstration, I ask the whole class to examine the essay on cheerleading. We very quickly agree that this writer has just skimmed the surface of the subject and has given us a rather flat picture of cheerleading. As a result, this essay could have been written by any high school cheerleader in the United States. We all agree that obviously cheerleading is important to this writer, but she doesn't give us sufficient detail to enter into her experience. I point out how important it would have been for this writer to hear the kind of things we are saying. Specific suggestions from her peers could have helped her to move her essay in a more productive direction during revision.

Providing Feedback

Though most students learn rather quickly how to talk appropriately about a piece of writing, I suggest to them that as writers and responders to writing, we need to be sure that we receive and give two specific kinds of feedback, reader-based and criterion-based (Elbow 1981). Criterion-based feedback is the kind we usually associate with what a teacher looks for in a piece of writing; i.e., how the writing stands up against a set of criteria, such as focus, paragraph development, sentence structure, agreement, etc. Reader-based feedback is a report on what is happening to readers, moment by moment, as they read a piece of writing; e.g., "My mind was wandering when you started, but when you got to the description of what it was that was making the terror rise in you, you grabbed my attention immediately." I encourage students to start with reader-based feedback because reader reaction is critical to the success of the paper. Subsequent criterion-based feedback then becomes more meaningful since audience response, on closer examination, is frequently affected or controlled by criterion-based factors.

Initially, my students usually have trouble giving both kinds of feedback. Therefore, before we move on to the next portion of the demonstration, I pass out a handout called a Group Response Guide, and we discuss it. I give my students these guides the first few times they work in peer revision groups. Each Group Response Guide is similar to the one below. Each contains five or six questions, mostly reader-based, though I do include some criterion-based questions. If the group is working smoothly, I tell them not to worry about answering all the questions on the handout. I use different questions on each guide, though the questions generally address similar issues. (The questions in the following guide were developed at Virginia Tech by Lou Middleman.)

Group Response Guide 1

Respond either orally or in writing (preferably both) to the following questions as they apply to each paper:

1. What things do you like best about the piece, and why are they good?

2. Is there anything that doesn't seem appropriately addressed to the intended audience? What, and why not?

3. Is there anything that makes you say "So what?" or "Specify!"? If so, put these words in the margins where you think they will be helpful.

4. In the margin, write "Say more," "Expand," "More details," or something like this at points where you as a reader need additional information in order to participate more fully in the event or the idea presented.

5. Underline words that are used improperly and phrases that don't seem to "make English." Place question marks above them.

6. How close to being ready to be turned in to a stranger for evaluation is this piece?

Circle one number: not ready 1 2 3 4 5 6 7 8 9 10 ready.

After we have examined and discussed the items on the sample Group Response Guide, I give my students a copy of a student essay that is relatively strong but still has problems that they can easily identify. I again assume the role of the writer of the essay, and this time I behave more rationally. The students in the demonstration group take their work seriously and try to give me useful feedback on what I supposedly have written. After this demonstration we discuss, as a class, what happened during the group session, including which behaviors were useful and which ones could have been or should have been avoided. After this discussion, I give my students a handout based on Ken Macrorie's "Reminders for Circlers" from *Writing to Be Read.* (Bob Boynton of Boynton/Cook Publishers kindly granted me permission to use this material.) This handout lists ten things for them to keep in mind while they are working in groups, such as their responsibility to give feedback, the need to avoid becoming defensive, the importance of dealing primarily with large issues, the need to focus on the writing in front of them instead of going off on a tangent, etc. I tell them to consider these items carefully and to think about each one in light of what they have observed during this demonstration session. I remind them that during the next class they will be working in peer revision groups for the first time, and that I want them to be prepared to use this time wisely.

Monitoring Student Progress

When students come to class for their first peer revision session, I usually take a few minutes to answer any questions they have about what they are supposed to do. I then divide the class into groups of three or four students and tell them to begin sharing their papers with each other. There are advantages and disadvantages in always having students work either in the same groups or in different ones. Some teachers carefully consider who will work with whom. It's up to you to decide how to handle group assignments. I prefer to choose the groups randomly at first and then make adjustments as necessary after students have worked together a while.

While the students are engaged in their group work, I wander around the room, constantly observing what is happening and listening to what is being said. When a group is in trouble or when they've reached a dead end for some reason, I intervene and give them some suggestions to get them working again. If I hear a student make a particularly cogent remark about another student's paper—

the kind of comment that can help them significantly revise their papers—I praise the person who made the comment and suggest that the writer might want to pay attention to what has just been said. After students have more experience, I occasionally join various groups as an active participant. I don't do this initially because my presence tends to inhibit interaction among students. However, after they are comfortable with the group situation and have gained confidence in giving and receiving feedback, they actually like and request my participation from time to time. As I work with these groups, I try to provide a positive model of how a person goes about giving useful feedback to writers about something they've written.

Follow-up Demonstrations

At the next class meeting after the first group session, I ask students to do a five-minute nonstop writing in which they tell me what worked or didn't work in their group. I collect these papers, read them, and give a summary of what was said the next day in class. I also give students some suggestions about what they can do to overcome difficulties they had. On the day before they are scheduled to work in groups again, I remind them of problems they had last time and, if necessary, demonstrate in some fashion how these problems can be overcome. I continue this follow-up procedure all year long, and as a result, my peer revision groups never deteriorate too far into something unproductive before I am able to get things going in the right direction again.

Conclusion

Getting students to work productively in peer revision groups is not an impossible task. If teachers show students what an effective revision group looks like, constantly monitor student progress as they learn how to engage in such collaboration, and follow up on any problem areas they or their students identify, there is no reason that peer revision can't become an integral part of every writing classroom, no matter what the level.

References

Elbow, P. 1981. *Writing with Power*. New York: Oxford University Press.
Macrorie, K. 1976. *Writing to Be Read*. 2nd ed. Rochelle Park, N.J.: Hayden.

17 Revising Response Groups

Marie Foley
University of California, Santa Barbara

Most instructors have encountered students for whom revision amounts to changing a word here and there, deleting an occasional wordy phrase, and checking cursorily for spelling errors. Their essays are usually drafted during an "all-nighter," and the revising, such as it is, takes place minutes before the final typing. By the time these students enroll in college composition, their well-entrenched revising habits need drastic revision. One could teach revision straightforwardly to the class, but in my opinion the best approach is to have students critique each other's rough drafts in response groups. Not only do such groups allow students to practice revising skills that will transfer to their own writing, but, as instructors who use them know, the group interaction can transform a class— generating a supportive environment and raising the class's overall level of achievement. To my mind, nothing works as well to create a sense in the classroom that writing matters.

Students with poorly developed revising strategies, however, cannot critique each other's work effectively. For response groups to work, students need training in how to revise and how to critique simultaneously. Over the years, I have tried a variety of training approaches, but none has effected the degree of change I wanted. What students need is a fundamental attitude change, because the gap between the way they revise and the way we expect them to revise is enormous. In her article comparing the revision strategies of students and of experienced writers, Nancy Sommers (1980) documents this gap. The students she interviewed describe their revising as "marking out words and putting different ones in" and "cleaning up the paper," while the professionals speak of "finding the argument," "taking apart what I have written," and "ask[ing] major theoretical questions" (pp. 381,84). A teaching technique is needed that bridges this gap, that radically transforms students' attitudes toward

117

revision and at the same time trains them to respond effectively in groups.

Donald Murray's (1978) proposal that the revising process be treated as a two-stage process—internal revision and external revision—suggested to me a possible answer. In his words, internal revision is the stage at which writers "discover and develop what they have to say"; later, during external revision, they "pay attention to the conventions of form and language, mechanics and style" (p. 91). Though such a division surely oversimplifies the writing process, it raises a possibility: why not establish two kinds of response groups analogous to internal and external revision? For each essay assigned, students would participate in two different groups, the first to pose "major theoretical questions" and the second to focus on stylistic concerns. The approach would automatically delay the polishing stage and force students to revise in the root sense of the word—to "re-see."

These two-stage response groups have proven highly successful in all levels of writing courses, from remedial to advanced. I call the two groups "work-in-progress groups" and "editing groups."

Work-in-Progress Sessions

At work-in-progress sessions, students divide into groups of three to read each other's rough drafts and respond to them verbally and in writing. As with all group activities, it is vital to conduct a modeling session beforehand. I pass around copies of a rough draft from a previous course and invite each student to suggest one question to pose to the writer or one piece of advice to improve the essay. Out of this discussion, we establish some ground rules, such as to emphasize the positive, to be specific, and not to nitpick. I enforce one other rule strictly—there must be no, absolutely no, discussion of grammar, spelling, or word choice. Rather, the students are to think globally about the rough draft, to ask themselves big questions: is the essay convincing? Does it need more information or detail? Is it fresh and surprising, or a rehash of the obvious? Does the writer's purpose seem clear and consistent? Does the essay unfold logically, or does it meander?

It is at this modeling session that I introduce the question that lies behind all others—"So what?" This question hits home in a way that perplexed me at first, but I have come to see that it verbalizes the letdown students have felt but never dared admit after reading an essay. "So what?" implies that readers expect to feel something and to learn from what they read: they want to care about it. The question implies that writing is an act of communication between writer and reader, a transaction in which the writer implicitly agrees to make the reading worthwhile. For students who have primarily been writing to complete the assignment, bent mainly on reaching that five-hundred-word limit, "So what?" introduces a new perspective— that writing matters. Of course, I recommend that in their groups the students use a more polite phrasing, such as "Why did you decide to write on this topic?" But the brasher version becomes a handy catchphrase in the class, a kind of inside joke that helps transform the class into a community.

If, as Murray and countless other writers have reminded us, writing is a process of discovery, it doesn't necessarily follow that writers can spot their own discoveries. Often what is truly fresh, surprising, or intriguing remains untapped until another reader sees it. In their work-in-progress groups, students can be trained to discover what is valuable in each other's work. To explain what I mean by *discovering,* I usually present the class with several especially dull, very rough drafts from former students and challenge them to find something of worth, whether it's just the introduction or even the topic choice. To their amazement, they are able to discover potential in even the most unpromising essay. One student praises the detail in a paragraph, another points out good insights in the conclusion, and soon they have put together an essay that excites them. This warm-up reduces their fear of facing someone's hopeless or uninspired essay and not knowing any way to respond except to mumble "real interesting essay." Students learn that if they read with the expectation of finding something of value, they will find it.

The process of discovering and of posing global questions usually requires the discarding of large chunks of a rough draft. Instructors should be forewarned that students' resistance to large-scale discarding is extraordinary! And no wonder, when for years they've regarded their first draft as a closed piece of writing—their final thinking on the topic. Old habits die hard, and instructors have to persist; it takes several group sessions before students feel comfortable suggesting drastic revisions to each other. It helps to remind students often not to fall in love with their first drafts.

Editing Groups

In the second kind of response group, students work as real editors do in preparing a piece of writing for publication (in this case, *pub-*

lication means submission to the instructor). I schedule the editing groups two class meetings after the work-in-progress groups so that students have at least four days to revise their rough drafts and I have an intervening class period for writing instruction. In the editing groups, students focus especially on the paragraph and the sentence and put into practice our class work on cohesion, style, and diction. They spot where relationships need clarification and ideas need amplification, where the writing is too obvious or dull or understated. Again, I discourage mere correcting, on the premise that spelling and grammar are the writer's responsibility (although general warnings may be given, such as to check for fragments). Also, I alert students that should the essay need major rethinking, they may return to the kind of global questions they posed in the work-in-progress groups.

Editing groups could consist of two or three students, with each student editing one or two essays, but I have evolved a more intensive and collaborative system. I divide the class into five groups, each of which edits one essay. Thus, five students' essays are edited during the class period (allowing about forty minutes for the editing), with everyone having at least one opportunity to be edited during the term. Initially, I allow students to form their own groups, but if I notice cliques beginning to form, I set up the groups myself so as to create new interactions.

In each editing group, the "presenter" reads his or her essay aloud while the editors follow along on photocopies. Oral reading, so vital to the polishing process, is one reason that I prefer the large editing groups to one-on-one editing; the noise of five simultaneous readings is tolerable, but twelve or more would be cacophonous. Reading aloud permits the editors to digest the text more slowly and, more importantly, to attend to the sounds and rhythms of the prose. They discover how much the ear picks up what the eye misses. The editors respond in writing on their copies, and then whoever finishes first begins discussing his or her responses with the presenter. Gradually all five editors join the discussion, which often becomes quite animated as they compare their responses. Since the editing day is also the due date for the essays, all students turn in their essays *except* the presenters, who receive an extended due date for another revision. Thus, the reward for being subject to editing scrutiny is the chance to turn in a better essay and get a higher grade.

Although only the five presenters receive the immediate grade benefit, all students in fact benefit, not only through the reinforcement of class exercises but more subtly in what they discover about closure. As students spot more and more possibilities for improving an essay, they are less ready to call their own work finished. If their classmate's essay—already a second or third draft—still has room for improvement, so must theirs. And though they don't in fact revise each essay to perfection, they are at least aware of its incompleteness. They begin to experience what Valéry said about writing poetry—that a piece of writing is never finished, it is just abandoned.

Conclusion

The main benefit of using two-stage response groups is that they break up the revision process, forcing students to take more time and invest more care in revision. These group sessions consume a lot of class time; in effect, they make revision the focus of the course. Students come to realize that revision is what writing is all about. Instead of writing a single draft at the last minute and hurriedly correcting it, they produce a quick first draft in which they let their ideas flow, regarding this draft as raw material to be shaped. As one student put it, "I just try to throw together my ideas so I can see what sort of direction to take." And another: "After I write my first draft, I take a step back. What am I really trying to say? I look for problems in flow, structure, style, and logic. Then I write a second draft that is *very* different from the first." As these end-of-term comments indicate, students eventually internalize the global questions they have posed in the work-in-progress groups. They begin to sound like Sommers's experienced adult writers, asking themselves major questions and re-visioning their own work, even before submitting it to their peers.

Let me repeat that this turnaround takes time; the first group sessions seldom produce dramatic changes because resistance to change is strong. Even with the carefully planned modeling sessions designed to elicit the responses I'm looking for, I often don't see new attitudes until midterm, and for some students not until the end of the term. But it is gratifying to see the changes take place, to watch students grow through these response groups into more mature, self-confident writers and editors, and to watch the class develop a mutual trust that allows them to become a supportive writing community.

References

Murray, D. 1978. Internal Revision: A Process of Discovery. *In Research on Composing: Points of Departure*, ed. C. R. Cooper and L. Odell. Urbana, Ill.: National Council of Teachers of English.

Sommers, N. 1980. Revision Strategies of Student Writers and Experienced Adult Writers. *College Composition and Communication* 31: 378–88.

18 Project Write Start: Elementary and Secondary Writing Partners

Kirsten Barfod Levinsohn and John Kendall
Rutgers Preparatory School
Somerset, New Jersey

A pair of long legs scrunch under a primary school desk and provide just enough room for a pair of much shorter legs to dangle freely. Between the two bodies lie a few pieces of paper, the focus of their attention. Alex, the younger student, is animatedly talking and gesticulating as Linda, his older partner, listens with serious consideration and, at times, amusement. She responds to her younger partner's ideas by sifting through ambiguities, encouraging depth, or laughing heartily. After further discussion, Linda begins to write down their collective ideas, stopping occasionally to ask Alex a question or to clarify a point. The talking and writing flow.

About twenty minutes later, after editing their collaborative effort, Linda and Alex proudly read their story to the hushed room. Responding to the applause of their classmates, they display broad smiles simultaneously. A few other pairs of writers share their stories, until the clock signals the end of the period. After bidding farewell to his partner, Alex approaches his second-grade teacher still clutching his story and implores, "Can we please do that again?"

Project Write Start began as a single joint writing experience between John Kendall's eleventh/twelfth-grade writing class and Kirsten Levinsohn's second-grade class, but quickly grew into a series of flesh-and-blood collaborations as the year progressed. The enthusiasm and creative prose generated from our first meeting convinced us to continue with the paired writings. By the end of the academic year, with half a dozen correspondences and four in-class visits, the two classes had yielded a tremendous array of verbal activity and had demonstrated improved abilities and confidence as well.

This project began with the celebration of Children's Book Week in November by Kirsten's Lower School* students. After the second graders read and discussed stories, created and "published" their own prose, and wrote to their favorite authors, John was invited to talk to them about his experiences as a published children's author.

When planning the details of the visit, however, we realized that tremendous potential for a writing project existed in the combined efforts of John's expository writing class and Kirsten's second graders. Thus, as an additional spur to literary activity, we planned to have the Upper School and Lower School students meet and work in pairs to compose a story.

Prior to the meeting, each second grader planned and drew a three-segmented picture outline of the story. The first drawing illustrated the character's problem, the second picture demonstrated the character's attempt to solve the problem, and the third frame showed whether the solution worked. Armed with these pictorial outlines, the second graders invited the Upper School students to their room. The older students then acted as scribes, taking down what the young authors dictated; as facilitators, encouraging clear and thoughtful responses; and as light-handed editors, fleshing out an occasional wobbly thought.

The mutual excitement and ambitious responses delighted us. Although we circled among the writers, braced for numerous cries for help, the students barely requested our services. Afterward, the teenage scribes neatly recopied the stories for homework, while their Lower School collaborators illustrated the stories and bound the text into a book. Feeling like budding Maxwell Perkinses, we displayed the finished works in the Upper School and Lower School libraries, before installing them as part of Kirsten's permanent classroom library.

Encouraged by the success of the fall collaborative writing experience, we planned other paired writing adventures. Although John had a new writing class in the second semester, Kirsten's seasoned veterans eagerly volunteered to break in the green recruits. Provided with a chance to start from scratch, we expanded the writing partnerships over several months with both long-distance and in-class writing.

To emphasize the fading art of letter writing, we began the class interaction with a pen pal assignment. Since we had found that the older students provided considerable motivation for the younger students, John's advanced expository writing class introduced them-

---

Lower School and *Upper School* refer to divisions of Rutgers Preparatory School.

selves via letters first. These were one-page letters telling where the teenagers lived, what they did in their free time, and how they saw life as sixteen-year-olds. We used individual file folders with both students' names on them as permanent "envelopes" to ensure independence from the group and to initiate partnerships between the pairs of writers. Lower Schoolers began to embellish their folders with drawings and doodles, and soon the teenagers began to draw in response, many of them requesting crayons or markers from John to compensate for being "underprivileged" Upper Schoolers armed only with pencils and ballpoints.

The second graders eagerly and impatiently awaited their pen pals' letters. They loved the personal attention from the older students; many would strut around the room with their prized letters, boasting of the letters' length, a particularly fine picture, or one of the accomplishments of their pen pals. Their letters of response often imitated the letters they had received, with similar syntax, form, or expressions of speech. In many cases, apparently wishing to show the importance of their own statements and to demonstrate their growing writing skills, the seven year-olds matched the length of their pen pals' letters.

Since storytelling worked well in the fall, we repeated a variation of that assignment for the first in-class meeting of this group of partners. This time, each student prepared for the joint meeting by writing a story's beginning, which introduced the characters, established the setting, and described the problem to be solved. Although Kirsten's second graders welcomed their heretofore unseen pen pals into their classroom with excited and nervous anticipation, friendly chatter soon ensued.

After reading their story introductions to each other, the pen pals switched them with each other. Each student then wrote the middle of his or her partner's story, elaborating on the dimensions of the problem described in the introduction and creating a way for the character to solve that problem. With much bantering back and forth, and a couple of fudge cookies for sustenance, the stories began to develop interesting twists and subplots that their originators never expected. The partners then returned the story's new middle to the surprised, delighted, and, at times, perplexed original storytellers. These writers then wrote the ending to the stories they began, and we concluded our first spring visit with the oral sharing of the pairs' mutual creativity. Kirsten added the recopied, illustrated, and bound drafts of these three-part stories to her classroom library.

Following two more exchanges of pen pal letters, we began another, more ambitious writing adventure, the creation of an "omegabet" (as opposed to an alphabet). We had already rejected several topics because of unsuitability. Through an "alphabet/omegabet" project, the students would examine the basic units of written language and experiment with the very abstract ideas behind the twenty-six letters.

First, each class read Rudyard Kipling's "How the Alphabet Was Made," a fictionalized account of how a caveperson invented the alphabet, and Dr. Seuss's *On Beyond Zebra,* a model for our own efforts.

Second, as a prewriting word-play activity, Kirsten gave her kids a vertical strip of the alphabet and asked them to write one or two words that began with each letter of the alphabet (e.g., "angry aardvarks," "bouncing balls"). Their Upper School pen pals then had to complete the phrases using an inverted alphabet (i.e., A matched Z, B matched Y, and so on, as in "Angry aardvarks are zealous," "Bouncing balls are never yellow," etc.). We then taped the written phrases to construction paper, attached them to fishing line, and hung the alphabet mobiles from John's classroom ceiling in time for the next visit of Lower Schoolers.

The omegabet arose from each second grader coining a new letter, drawing it, and inventing a new word or words that used the new letter, just as Dr. Seuss does in his story. The Upper Schoolers helped the second graders compose a story involving the new letters and words. For example, Aparna made the letter "ahik" and with her teenage partner, Robert, composed the following explanation:

This letter stands for Miss A/Khookia doodle. It's the ancestor of archeopteroy (a dinosuar). It makes a chicken noise. She has a very long tail. And a very short beak. Her feathers are purple and pink. She has turquoise wings. And the left of her body is red. She likes to fly . . . She drinks fruit punch. She has 3 children: Mary, Carol and George.

Michael created the letter "eeck" and with his Upper School partner, Joe, explained its origin:

An eeck stands for a dust storm in Antartica. This dust storm kills all the penguins whether good or bad. It covers sixteen miles at a time. The eeck turns the penguins into carrots, not fancy carrots but orange ones. Eskimos, who would disappear if caught in the storm, come and eat all the carrots that used to be penguins.

We assembled our fifteen newly invented letters, complete with stories and pictures, and provided all thirty partners and the two school libraries with our own version of *On Beyond Zebra*.

Originally, we had planned to end Project Write Start with the creation of the omegabet. However, both classes had enjoyed the exchanges immensely, and they pleaded for one more visit. Although only two weeks of school remained, we couldn't resist their enthusiasm and used one Upper Schooler's suggestion of a cartoon strip collaboration. We photocopied several pages of small stick figures in various action poses from a how-to-draw book. Each partner selected four or five figures before the paired visit, and was required to use at least one of their figures in the joint cartoon strip. We then rejoined forces a final time, provided blank "storyboards," and the fifteen pairs of partners went to work to create cartoon narratives. Their humorous efforts were shared, photocopied, and displayed on a bulletin board; this allowed students and visitors alike the opportunity for a good chuckle.

Throughout our many paired writing activities, the enthusiasm on both sides of the campus always ran high as a result of careful planning and the very nature of cooperative learning. We always spent considerable time beforehand constructing activities that would challenge both the Lower Schoolers and, in a different way, the Upper Schoolers. Kirsten would frequently "prewrite" with her kids through reading stories, discussing ideas, and assigning related literary activities. John would explain to his students the overall intent of an activity but would often use the spontaneity of the class meeting and the intensity of completing the collective assignment within the class period to kindle interest and to provide challenge. We met for forty minutes, which included brief introductions or explanations, a sizable block of time for composing, and then a ten-minute cookie break and oral sharing of the fruits of the students' literary labors. John's kids would then recopy the work more legibly, while Kirsten's students would illustrate the stories or make book covers for them.

Along with preparation, the other important contribution to the success of our writing collaborations stemmed from the intrinsic benefit of student-to-student motivation, inspiration, and creation. Kirsten's second graders were thrilled to see their own ideas take such form and length. For so long their imaginations had been held in check by their slower and less advanced fine motor skills. At their age, these students' ideas had always blazed ahead of their struggling pencils on paper. Now their more experienced "chauffeurs" enabled them to translate their mental words into physical words faster and more effectively. The second graders were delighted to see their ideas being accepted so readily by their older partners and were intrigued to see how those same ideas were slightly remodeled and polished to make for a more cogent and smoother story. With their partners, they added descriptors, crossed out irrelevant details, and, at times, struggled to find the right language to create the desired effect.

Shifted into the role of primary literacy experts, John's students also enjoyed and learned from the experience. The unfolding stories and their younger partners' intensity often amused them. But the effort of rewording without interfering, guiding without inhibiting, and teaching without preaching provided a unique challenge. For most students, this was their first teaching experience. Many found that they had to resist the temptation to completely overhaul their partners' stories or, at the other extreme, to ignore the ambiguities and the inconsistencies because the literary faults were too hard to explain. Often the older students' faces betrayed their difficulties in figuring out how to facilitate the mutual reworking of the pieces. The uplifted, eager, and trusting faces of their partners helped them to make that pedagogical plunge. Moreover, these attempts at guiding the writing of their younger partners increased the teenagers' own metacognitive awareness of what constitutes good prose.

In addition, many of the teens realized the mixed blessings of adulthood through their return to an elementary classroom. They loved the nostalgic regression into childhood: they argued intensely about morning snack, demanded wide-lined paper and fat pencils for recording, and lobbied against censorship from the adult teachers. Indeed, many tried on the shoes of censorship themselves for the first time as they tried to wean their partners from preoccupation with Rambo, killer robots, and maniacal monsters (with only minimal success).

Perhaps in nine or ten years, it will be Alex's turn to scrunch long legs under a desk in the Lower School, and he will collaborate with a pen pal yet to be born. Some of his classmates will remember the experience permanently, especially with a thick file folder of letters and several class projects to remind them. Just as Linda's class may become more sophisticated editors and more sensitive adults through the experience, we hope that Alex will still be as excited about writing as he was after the first collaboration.

References

Dr. Seuss. 1980. *On Beyond Zebra.* New York: Random House.

Kipling, R. 1974 [1902]. *Just So Stories.* New York: NAL.

IV Additional Collaborative Learning Activities

19 A Lesson in Rhetoric: Writing and Performing TV Commercials

G. Douglas Meyers
University of Texas at El Paso

There is no doubt that the television commercial has changed—and will continue to change—the way we fit into the world. The average youngster between the ages of five and eighteen, according to Neil Postman (1987), sees approximately one thousand television commercials each week. We can safely assume, then, that our students are well acquainted with this ubiquitous genre. While most English teachers lament the disproportionately large amount of time that students stay fixed in front of the tube, we are also growing increasingly interested in making connections between the TV "curriculum" and some of our own teaching goals.

There are many ways to exploit television advertising to improve students' abilities as critical thinkers, speakers, listeners, readers, and writers. A definite correspondence exists, for instance, between TV commercials and any other piece of intentional communication that uses language. Much contemporary theory emphasizes the rhetorical nature of *all* communication—that it occurs for specific purposes, in specific contexts, with specific audiences and writers/speakers engaged—and many parallels can be drawn between the rhetoric of the TV commercial and the rhetoric of writing. Particularly when students lack a sense of purpose, or audience, or understanding of occasion in their writing and therefore grind out arhetorical "Engfish," the TV commercial makes a provocative pedagogical tool. And because most students are already accustomed to responding publicly and collectively to the electronic media, TV commercials are a "natural" for group work.

The cooperative learning activity described here is predicated upon several commonsense teaching principles: (1) that students can take responsibility for their own learning when engaged as active learners in small groups, (2) that the most effective learning takes place when we build on what we can already do well in order to develop new competencies and to raise consciousness, and (3) that teachers can best facilitate learning by articulating objectives specifying definite tasks and outcomes. This activity is also *integrative*—bridging gaps between speaking and writing, skills and imagination—and by introducing dramatic activities into the English classroom, it encourages learning that is creative and entertaining.

Implementation and Materials

By calling off numbers around the room, students are randomly assigned to work in a group with three other classmates. This procedure mixes students by varying levels of ability and achievement, sex, and ethnic background, an arrangement that creates a "we're all in this together" camaraderie promoting the exchange of different ideas.

The instructor gives the following directions:

> Each group will choose one card from each of these three different stacks of index cards. Using the information on your three cards, your group will work together to write a script for a TV commercial to advertise a product to be bought as a present for a certain type of person for a specific gift-giving occasion. You will be able to use the rest of today's class to work on your script—to figure out what your product is and how you might advertise it for your specific audience and occasion. It might be wise to have a recorder for each group so you don't lose track of your ideas. Tomorrow, each group will act out their commercial at the front of the classroom. If you want to use any props, you can bring them in then. Your finished commercial should last approximately one minute, and every member of your group should somehow be involved in its presentation.

Each group chooses one card (folded, to prevent reading before choosing) from each of the following sets of cards (which the instructor has prepared ahead of time):

Hypothetical Product Names. These names are invented with a connotative potential in mind, so that students can create whatever product seems appropriate for the sound and look of the word. One of the first major rhetorical decisions that students must make, in fact, is at the level of word choice and style: what product could this particular name represent appropriately? Some of the Hypothetical Product Name cards I have used include "Sparkum," "9.5," "McNamara's," "Onadi," "Ravot," "Le Bon," "Mañana," "Termo," "dan-dan's," "Fancredible," and "ZYX."

Gift Recipients. These cards identify the secondary audiences whom students must implicitly address in their commercials—the people for whom the gift is intended. The primary audience to whom students are marketing their product is *not* the recipients themselves but people who buy gifts *for* the recipients. Students are thus presented with a rather challenging rhetorical problem, that of accommodating hierarchical audiences. They must brainstorm about who these people are and what kinds of commercials might win them over, inventorying the emotions and characters of their audiences and identifying the kinds of appeals and lines of argument that might persuade them—the stuff of Aristolelean rhetoric. Some of the Gift Recipient cards I have used include Mother, Father, Brother, Sister, Daughter, Son, Grandfather, Grandmother, Granddaughter, Grandson, Boyfriend, Girlfriend, Boss, Graduate, Teacher, and Self.

Occasions for Gift Giving. These cards suggest a context for the gift-giving occasion, the cluster of connotations and denotations associated with a particular celebrated day. Students must explore the nuances of this specific occasion, since one main purpose of this assignment is to create just the right pitch for the right people at the right time. Some of the Occasion cards I have used include Birthday, Valentine's Day, Mother's Day, Father's Day, Anniversary, Fourth of July, Christmas, Hanukkah, Halloween, Graduation, Retirement, Moving, and "Just Because."

Procedure

Having selected their cards, students work together to generate fresh material for their commercial. This activity emphasizes the creativity and serious playfulness that characterize successful inventional strategies. By discouraging the application of rigid rules (something that often disables poor composers), the commercial-composing colloquy promotes flexibility and the exploration of many rhetorical choices: together, students discover and create content, arrangement, and style, as well as voice, tone, and point of view. They come to understand the constraints of the rhetorical problem they are grappling with and the implications of the choices they make in solving that problem. They imaginatively and animatedly improvise, trying out different solutions. At one minute the product is defined as such-and-such, and the next minute it is something quite different; for a second, a certain advertising appeal is thought to be effective, and a moment later it is rejected for its lack of suitability for the occasion. Because this is a group activity, the decisions are *reasoned* decisions—ones that engage students in stating and defending their opinions about different rhetorical matters.

The variety of specific rhetorical problems is large, for students in each group are involved in developing a unique communication. Yet all groups must focus on the same variables: content (the product), purpose (to sell), audience, and occasion. The group attempting to develop a commercial aimed at persuading people to give "Sparkum" to Grandma for her birthday is trying to accomplish something identical to, yet different from, the group writing the commercial aimed at getting viewers to buy their boyfriends "Onadi" for the Fourth of July or their sisters "9.5" for Valentines's Day. Even when students get a seemingly nonsensical combination of cards, (for example, giving "Ravot" to Grandpa on Graduation Day or giving "ZYX" to Teacher upon Retirement), the activity works well *because* of the incongruities the students must consciously address in designing their commercials.

Sharing and Responding

Invariably, each group has great fun hamming it up in front of their classmates, performing their original TV commercial. Usually all cast members are motivated enough to know their lines by heart, and often props are brought in to make the sixty-second spot visually appealing.

Immediately after each commercial is presented, all members of the class (including the instructor) write several sentences of feedback to give to the group members at the end of the class period, commenting on the commercial and making special note of the success with which it made the invented product attractive to its intended audience for the intended occasion. Once all the commercials have been acted out, a large class discussion ensues, highlighting the importance of audience, purpose, and occasion for any communication. Students now have much to say about these elements of rhetoric, thanks to both the new insight and the increased availability of prior knowledge that this exercise makes possible.

Depending on other course objectives, this activity can be used as a springboard for further group exploration of the connections between nonprint media and written composition. For example, instructors might want to address such topics as the types of reasoning and organizational patterns in visual and verbal forms of composition, the "grammar" of the electronic media versus the grammar of language, and verbal transitions versus visual transitions. Having enacted an amateur commercial, students may be assigned to analyze professional advertisements, examining how they use different types of claims, warrants, and evidence. Time might also be devoted to studying how the scripts could be revised into effective pieces of expository prose.

Regardless of what follows this cooperative learning project, my experience tells me that this activity, by itself, delivers important lessons in rhetoric to students. It helps to sensitize them to issues of audience, purpose, and occasion; it emphasizes the power of using language economically (the commercials last for only one minute); it refines their ability to make defensible rhetorical choices; and it encourages them to talk to and to listen to one another. It may even prepare them to deal more critically with the more than fifty thousand commercials they will view during the coming year.

Reference

Postman, N. 1987. *Teaching as a Conserving Activity.* New York: Dell.

20 The Sound of Music: A Harmonious Meeting of Minds

Virginia McCormick
Allen High School
Allentown, Pennsylvania

Dust as we are, the immortal spirit grows
Like harmony in music; there is a dark
Inscrutable workmanship that reconciles
Discordant elements, makes them cling together
In one society.

Wordsworth, *The Prelude*, Book 1, l. 340ff.

Rogers and Hammerstein's *The Sound of Music* begins with the familiar words "The hills are alive with the sound of music. . . ." And alive with sound is just what a classroom is when a teacher undertakes group projects. Many teachers are reluctant to attempt group work because of the potential resulting chaos. But dissonance can be turned into harmony.

What evokes more dread in the hearts of English teachers everywhere than having to teach—not assign, but *teach*—the research paper? Couple that monumental task with the additional requirement of teaching it to the average-ability eleventh-grade student, and most English teachers query with a faint-of-heart "Who, me?" Always the optimist, I decided that since the paper had to be taught, I must find some palatable way of motivating a class of thirty-two girls and three boys—few, if any, of whom were planning to attend college. How could I convince them that they must write a research paper as a part of the requirement for junior-year English? While I could simply announce, "Do it or fail," I chose not to because I wanted them to understand the process, and I wanted their research to become a worthwhile learning experience. After ruminating about the dilemma for some time, I decided upon a solution I hoped would be challenging and instructive: combine group work with research.

Some time ago I was enchanted by the idea of Steve Allen's television program "Meeting of Minds." For those unfamiliar with the program, Steve Allen created round-table discussions to which he invited notable guests: Michelangelo, Socrates, Leonardo DaVinci, Catherine the Great, Voltaire, Thomas Paine, William Blake, Emily Dickinson, Elizabeth Barrett Browning, Oliver Cromwell, the Empress Theodora, Attila the Hun, and Bertrand Russell. A discussion would feature three to four guests, each of whom was introduced individually. Dialogue progressed between the moderator and one guest, the two guests, and so forth, until each of the chairs was occupied. At this point, some lively discussion ensued, featuring philosophical or moral questions indicative of or reflective of each guest's era and culture. Some bickering, some applause, some guffaws would occur, but what prevailed for the viewer was a new perspective of time and space.

Before I informed my students about the impending research paper requirements, I let them view an episode of "Meeting of Minds." They became so fascinated with Catherine the Great's romantic escapades and Oliver Cromwell's rage over his musical introduction ("God Save the King") that they were eager to find out how this program related to English class.

Next, I enticed the class with a little theatricality. When they entered the classroom the next day, they found sealed 9″ × 12″ manila envelopes labeled "MISSION: POSSIBLE" on their desks. They were cautioned not to open them. As the bell for class rang, I played a recording of the theme song from the TV show "Mission: Impossible." Sufficiently intrigued, the students opened their packets. Each packet contained information about research skills: time lines, procedures, footnote and bibliography guidelines, notetaking information, and general format rules, as well as instructions for selecting one of thirty famous people. After I reviewed procedures and contents of the packet, I invited students to form groups and choose the name of a famous person from the list of thirty.* I explained that each group would explore one famous person's life and times. Secondly, the completed papers would be culled, and from them would come a script for our own version of "Meeting of Minds." Excitement flashed through the room. Students then grouped themselves, and each group chose a person to investigate. From the list of thirty

---

*I would be happy to share these materials with anyone who would like to have them. Write me at Allen High School, 17th and Turner Streets, Allentown, PA 18104.

famous men and women, the groups chose Pocahontas, Shirley Temple, Helen Keller, Laura Ingalls Wilder, and Linda Ronstadt.

Next I asked each group to complete a survey detailing the names of the group members, the name of the chosen famous person, and other critical information. For this survey, each group member selected an area of interest to investigate so that he or she could become familiar with the person's life and times. The areas of investigation included autobiographical/biographical information, historical/political events, medical/scientific/technological advances, socioeconomic climate, artistic/cultural endeavors, and current events pertinent to each person and time period being investigated.

Research

Students began researching their topics and persons and soon had accumulated bibliography cards and note cards. After I checked both types of cards to make sure students were on the right track, I suggested that each group brainstorm in order to decide *how* to explain the person's life and times in the most reasonable and efficient manner. After students had devised a simple outline, I suggested that they divide it into sections and that each person in the group take a section. Now they had a real challenge. Because most students chose to develop their papers chronologically rather than as narrative (the two forms of biography and autobiography we had learned about earlier in the year), they could not use just the note cards each one had filled out. They needed other information. In other words, each student was dependent upon the others in his or her group for careful notetaking. If Johnny didn't take good notes about the historical events during Helen Keller's lifetime, Suzy would have to backtrack and investigate again. Because students didn't want to let down their fellow group members, they took copious and thorough notes. They actually spent hours after school and on Saturdays at the public library working out kinks in their chronology. The collaborative effort was thorough, and the group members worked together to produce a whole and harmonious paper. As each group wrote its paper, members challenged, encouraged, chided, and cooperated with one another on such academic matters as choice of transitional phrases, legibility of work, coherence of writing, word choice, and appropriateness of material. As a result of the collaborative effort, I received five excellent research papers.

Students had evidenced numerous skills, including functioning at all levels of Bloom's taxonomy.

Preparing for the Program

Next, five students volunteered to be scriptwriters. Their task was to take the five papers and, after reading them, determine what was important and what was extraneous. They had to synthesize the information and produce a script that showed each famous person's character, but they also had to decide upon what current issues to discuss at the roundtable. Although only five students actually wrote the script, they had plenty of advice—and criticism—from the rest of the class. One day I walked into class to hear Frank declare, "How could you possibly forget to discuss the impact TV has had on civilization? Where would Shirley Temple be without it? And who ever heard of Laura Ingalls Wilder before she got her own TV show?"

In the meantime, other groups of students organized other facets of the production. One group fashioned costumes; another learned about videotaping; another decided upon and found theme music for each character; another found props, located a stage, and checked on lighting; and the last group became actors and actresses.

Finally the script was written and duplicated, and the actors and actresses learned their parts. Interestingly, the writers allowed no one but the teacher and the actors and actresses to see the script before the production. They wanted everyone to be surprised.

The Great Minds Meet

On the day of the taping, the class assembled in the home economics living room, which had been transformed with cameras, lights, props, and music. The theme music began, and the announcer announced the program and guests. The host walked onto the set and made a few introductory remarks. Then he introduced a six-year-old Shirley Temple, who skipped in, curls bobbing, skirt bouncing, licking a giant lollipop, to the tune of "Baby, Take a Bow." After some preliminary discussion with Shirley about her career as a child star, the host introduced Pocahontas, who arrived to the beat of tom-toms. When Pocahontas's early life had been explored sufficiently, the host introduced Helen Keller and Annie Sullivan.

Students from the Helen Keller group had recognized that they had an additional problem. Since Helen Keller was blind, deaf, and mute, how could a panel communicate with her? They wanted Helen to participate in the discussion, but they knew that the audience's willing suspension of disbelief would be stretched to its limits if Helen were able to see, hear, and speak. Therefore, this group added Annie Sullivan, who spoke in a charming Irish brogue and interpreted for Helen, the panel, and the audience. The students who portrayed Helen and Annie were so concerned with authenticity that they had gone to the local Association for the Blind and learned some simple sign language. Appropriately enough, the music selected for Helen and Annie's entrance was "I Can See Clearly Now."

Next we met Linda Ronstadt, who was dressed in the latest fashion and entered to one of her hit songs, "Party Girl." After some preliminary biographical information, Linda questioned Shirley Temple about her show business career.

What a perfect cue for Laura Ingalls Wilder! Although Laura was never in show business, her writing of the Little House books enabled the creation of the popular TV show "Little House on the Prairie." Therefore, what better musical introduction could she have than the theme from the show based on her writing? The moderator questioned Laura briefly about her family, her schooling, and the hardships her family endured as pioneers on the frontier.

The subject of hardships produced a lively discussion among the group. The questions of Indian cruelty and cruelty *to* Indians arose and produced a number of insights about early pioneer life. The discussion then proceeded to societal views of handicaps. When Pocahontas indicated that a child with handicaps such as Helen Keller's would be isolated from the tribe and left somewhere to die, an irate Annie Sullivan pounded her clenched fist on the table and demanded an explanation. Pocahontas responded, saying that it was a tenet of her tribe's religion to cast aside anyone who could not take care of him- or herself. In addition, she said, the Creator did not expect anyone who was not perfect physically to live. This discussion continued with vehement arguments for some time as each member of the panel contributed her outrage about treatment or mistreatment of others, not only the handicapped. Before anyone realized it, the cameraman was signaling that the allotted time was nearly over.

Interestingly enough, one of the most positive contributions of the project for the class was that the young lady who portrayed Laura Ingalls Wilder was learning-disabled with a severe memory problem. Earlier in the year, class members had little to do with her, but as she undertook the part of Laura, her group and then the entire class became very supportive. While she did have some difficulty remembering her lines, she succeeded in her art as Laura and won the respect and admiration of her classmates.

Playing to a Wider Audience

The culmination of this experience was the viewing of the video-taped program on the last day of school. A number of guests were invited to the presentation. One of the most surprising outcomes of this project was that on the day of the viewing, teachers from all over the school, from a variety of disciplines, stopped by or called and asked when it was being shown. Apparently, the students were so enthusiastic, even the normally reticent ones, that they told any-one within earshot about their production. As a result, the screening had a large and varied audience.

What impressed most of the adults was the wholehearted involve-ment of the class during the viewing. Students anticipated certain parts of the script. They were eager to see Annie pound the table in disbelief about the treatment of the handicapped, and they were genuinely enthusiastic and supportive of the student who played Laura when she remembered her lines. The camaraderie exhibited throughout this venture into group research surpasses any I have experienced during my teaching career.

That was the first year's effort. Over the past four years, we've had visits from Albert Schweitzer, P. T. Barnum, Jim Thorpe, Elea-nor Roosevelt, Marie Antoinette (kids seem to like the challenge of dealing with the beheading of the grande dame), Gandhi, Galileo, Dolley Madison, Jacqueline Kennedy Onassis, Charlie Chaplin, Babe Ruth, Michelangelo, and Rasputin. We've had a great time and learned a lot. We've learned to respect individual rights, to work to-gether, and to research complex topics. We've managed to be cre-ative, to work the school's videotape equipment, and to find solu-tions to seemingly insurmountable problems. Most of all, however, we've found that we can still be individuals and work as a cohesive group to produce research papers and a videotape of our efforts.

Evaluation

Evaluation is always a difficult task for a teacher, and group work compounds that difficulty at least tenfold. After numerous attempts at grading this project, I devised the following system. Each student is graded individually on bibliography cards and note cards. After that, the group is graded on a point system for completion of each task. Quality does not seem to be a problem. Because of students' desire to have an A paper, each group member criticizes the rough draft of the paper and makes suggestions and improvements. I give students a checklist to verify specific elements before they submit their papers for grading.

In addition, as a check on shared responsibility I ask each student to keep and submit a process journal. From time to time, I collect and check journals to determine whether the group is working well together or whether someone is having a particular problem.

Throughout the group process, students are responsible to one another for finding accurate information. They must take good notes, and they must share tasks and be responsible workers. Ultimately, the project emphasizes each student's talents rather than his or her shortcomings. Better yet, it helps students analyze, synthesize, and evaluate what is important and what isn't. Many times I've overheard one student challenge another with "But [famous person's name] would *never* say that!"

Obviously students obtained information in their quest. Furthermore, they had to use comprehension skills in order to apply the information. In addition, students had to analyze and select specific portions of information to write their research papers. They then had to evaluate that information and synthesize it into a form other than the original text. Beyond that, the class had to use the same skills on a higher level of abstraction in order to produce a script and carry out their chore.

Conclusion

Group work is not neat and tidy in practice or in grading, in ideas or in noise level. It is usually chaotic and dissonant. Ann Berthoff (1981) encourages teachers to tolerate chaos when she says,

> Now, chaos is scary: the meanings that can emerge from it, which can be discerned taking shape within it, can be discovered only if students who are learning to write can learn to tolerate ambiguity. It is to our teacherly advantage that the mind doesn't like chaos; on the other hand, we have to be alert to the fact that meanings can be arrived at too quickly, the possibility of other meanings being too abruptly foreclosed. What we must realize ourselves and make dramatically evident to our students is what I. A. Richards means when he calls ambiguities "the hinges of thought." (pp. 70–71).

Yes, group work is chaotic and dissonant, but it fosters thinking and imagination. It helps us to "hinge" things together, to make associations and connections. Certainly the dusty immortal spirits we've conjured up in our research project help us to begin "a dark / Inscrutable workmanship that reconciles / Discordant elements, makes them cling together / In one society" to produce a harmonious "Meeting of Minds." No matter how harmonious or dissonant the groups of students involved in this project become, I will never forget the warning I overheard a senior give an incoming junior. "Every time you hear the sound of music in her class, look out! It means trouble, and boy, does it mean work!"

References

Berthoff, A. 1981. *The Making of Meaning: Metaphors, Models, and Maxims for Writing Teachers*. Montclair, N.J.: Boynton/Cook.

Wordsworth, W. 1967. *The Prelude*. In *English Romantic Writers*, ed. D. Perkins. New York: Harcourt Brace Jovanovich.

21 Six Sides to Learning

S. Phyllis M. Taufen, SNJM
Gonzaga University

Seven, come eleven—throw the dice! No, not classroom gambling but cooperative learning with a six-sided box. This activity challenges high school seniors as well as grade school learners—pushing all to see beyond the obvious. Built on individual and group planning, writing, and publishing, "Six Sides" encourages cooperative learning, fosters creativity, and spotlights both the individual and the group. A quick look at the what, the how, and the why of the activity will clarify this cooperative venture.

WHAT? Boxes displaying collaborative writing efforts are the final products of this group endeavor. Boxes—colorful and creative, piled on library shelves, hanging as mobiles, stacked on activity tables, and handled daily. Boxes—written and designed by student groups. Boxes—describing, narrating, analyzing; bringing together skills, cooperation, and learning.

HOW? Divide the class into groups of six students. Choose ordinary, familiar topics for student collaboration: peanut butter sandwiches, jogging shoes, locker keys, T-shirts, ice cream cones. Then direct the groups to select one object and imagine what it could be, what it could do, what caused it, who needs it, and what makes it *it*. They poke it, stretch it, cuddle it, listen to it, fight for it. Together, they brainstorm, listing facts and fantasies.

With this prewriting exercise finished, individuals throw the dice, rolling until everyone has a different number. ONE means describe the object; TWO, tell a story about the object; THREE, compare or contrast it; FOUR, find its causes (or effects); FIVE, classify or divide it; and SIX, argue for it.

With the luck of the throw, students write one hundred words or more on their object using the brainstorming list and the designated form: description, narration, comparison/contrast, cause/effect, classification, or argument. Working individually, they prepare their first drafts.

Returning to the group and working in twos or threes, the students rewrite and edit. When ready for the final draft, the group approves all six selections and decides on the format for publication: hand-printed in pencil, pen, or colored pens; calligraphy; word-processed copy; or whatever.

A shoe box makes a sturdy base for the polished product. Throw away the lid and cut the box in half, crosswise. Shove the two ends together, turning the first end upside down to fit inside the second. Tape. Cut paper to fit the sides, transcribe the six short selections into the desired format, and paste the selections onto the box. (If shoe boxes are scarce, gather graham cracker boxes or ask the athletic department for volleyball cartons.) When finished, the cubes are presented to the class, critiqued, displayed on shelves and tables, hung from lights, and enjoyed for weeks on end.

Who can resist picking up the "Six Sides of an Ice Cream Cone" and reading one author's classification section:

> Ice cream cones can be classified in several ways. When it comes to size, you can order one scoop, two, or even three if you can keep them piled atop your cone. Size can be more than three scoops if you want, but take your dog or little brother along to eat what hits the sidewalk.
>
> Also, cones can be classified according to color, and they vary from pecan peach to black licorice. In between you have a rainbow of red raspberry, orange sherbet, yellow lemon, green pistachio, fresh blueberry, or purple blackberry.
>
> Look out, however, for an ice cream cone is also dangerous and falls into the annoying, embarrassing, or painful class. It can run through your fingers, down your arm, and make you sticky all afternoon. It can be embarrassing and dribble down your new shirt or slacks and then plop on the car seat. Worst of all, if eaten too fast, an ice cream cone can zoom to a spot above your right eye and give you a jabbing headache.
>
> So beware of these facts next time you say, "Let's go get an ice cream cone."

Or who can pick up the cube giving six aspects of a locker key and read only once the comparison/contrast side printed there:

> A locker key can be compared to many things. In size, it is smaller than most car keys, a credit card, and a half-eaten chocolate chip cookie. It is, however, bigger than a dime, most buttons (except some designer ones), and a life saver.

When it comes to hardness, a locker key beats a plastic spoon, cardboard, or even my fried hamburgers. Put up against aromas, it loses all contests with cut grass, summer rains, opening a new can of coffee, or my mom's perfume. It wins, though, with negative smells like cooked liver, the garbage can, and my lunch from last month in the bottom of my locker.

In usefulness, however, my locker key beats most entries. It can safely hide my posters, last year's science project, gym shoes, tardy slips I haven't taken home, and the latest note from you-know-who. Part of my life is secret and safe because of this tiny key.

And finally, WHY? Cooperative learning flourishes with "Six Sides." Working together to see the many facets of an object sets a common goal and directs the process, giving space and time for frequent interaction and learning. Brainstorming and sharing ideas energizes everyone and gives even the weaker student a good list for starters. Rewriting and editing together in small groups provides mutual support and enables students to utilize key skills. Because the box requires six sides, individual contributions are important and are kept intact—not discarded or swallowed up in a group summary. And when someone is needed to make the box, choose the colors, or create that special touch, cooperation and learning continue.

Finally, building the box demands the skills, discipline, generosity, and growth inherent in cooperative learning. Seeing ideas in three dimensions—to be touched, turned, and enjoyed—makes important both the product and the process, the individual and the group.

Teachers adept at presenting material, forming groups, and monitoring progress will find "Six Sides" adaptable and suited to many age levels. However, one problem sparking heated debates and yet to be resolved remains: "Who gets to take the box home?" Maybe throwing dice again is the only solution!

22 Literature across the Curriculum: *The Twenty-One Balloons* in the Sixth-Grade Classroom

Donald R. Bear
Center for Learning and Literacy
University of Nevada–Reno

Deborah Lohman
Shoreham-Wading River Middle School
Shoreham, New York

The Twenty-One Balloons is a fantasy that has appeal for teachers and students alike. For teachers, especially toward the end of the school year, the book's major character is an inspiration. After forty years as an arithmetic teacher, Professor William Waterman Sherman makes plans to spend a year traveling in a balloon: "In this giant balloon he thought he could float around for a whole year, out of touch with the earth, with nobody to bother him and leaving his destination to the winds" (p. 5).

At Shoreham-Wading River Middle School, the book served as a springboard for an integrated unit of study on world cultures and geography. This unit also included lessons on letter and report writing, notetaking, and preparing bibliographies, as well as science lessons on water desalinization and the principles involved in balloon travel. The students enjoyed the story, worked together on their various projects, and prepared with their parents an international festival.

The Twenty-One Balloons, published in 1947 and available in paperback, was a Newbery Award winner and is but one of William Pène Du Bois's books. Since, as Flannery O'Connor said, a good story resists paraphrase, the gist of the story is provided:

In 1883, Professor Sherman leaves San Francisco in the *Globe*. A sea gull punctures the balloon, and the professor is rescued by one of the residents on the rumbling Pacific island of Krakatoa, located between Java and Sumatra. The island is filled with diamond mines,

151

and the twenty families who have been selected to live there are the richest in the world.

The families are named after letters of the alphabet, and each family has four members; for example, Mr. A, Mrs. A, and a boy and a girl named A-1 and A-2. The island is governed by a Gourmet Constitution, and the inhabitants follow a Restaurant Calendar. There are twenty days to a month. Each day of the month, one family is responsible for preparing meals for the other residents. Each family has adopted the ways of a country that begins with their letter. Their homes are restaurants designed in the architectural style of the particular country, and they serve the food of that country:

> The A.'s run an American restaurant and serve only real American cooking. You are now eating at the B.'s. This is a British chop house. The C.'s run a Chinese restaurant. The D.'s run a Dutch restaurant, the E.'s an Egyptian restaurant. . . . (p. 88)

The residents have designed many wonderful inventions, including a craft lifted by twenty balloons that is to be used should the volcano erupt. This is just what happens, and everyone boards the craft. Most of the inhabitants drop to safety over India. Left alone, Professor Sherman ditches the craft just off the coast of England, fifteen days after he left San Francisco.

Professor Sherman is rescued and suddenly becomes a worldwide celebrity. Everyone wonders how he could have made the trip in such a short time. The book actually begins with Professor Sherman's account of his journey before the members of the Western American Explorers' Club.

As some may know, the volcano on Krakatoa did erupt in 1883, and was heard three thousand miles away. Over one hundred thousand people died from the tidal waves. PBS's "Nature" has had a special on Krakatoa, and scientists have been interested in how the island became inhabited after the explosion.

In New York State, where sixth graders study world geography and history, the possibilities for using this book in a core or integrated curriculum are enormous, and over the past three years we have developed a number of cooperative learning activities that involve small-group presentations, team teaching, and parents.

The unit is designed to last anywhere from six to nine weeks. Before the unit begins we look at the district's curricula to see how the various content goals and language arts objectives can be incorporated. There are three basic components to this unit. The first component involves listening comprehension and notetaking activities two or three times a week. The second and third components are projects in which students focus on research skills and expository writing. The projects involve small-group work sessions several times a week. The listening comprehension and notetaking activities and the projects are run concurrently because as students read the book they develop ideas for different projects. For the sake of convenience in exposition, however, the three strands will be discussed separately in the following sections.

Listening Comprehension and Notetaking

The first four chapters of *The Twenty-One Balloons* are read to the students using a Directed Listening-Thinking Activity (DL-TA) format (Stauffer 1975). Prior to each reading session, the teacher marks appropriate stopping points where the students will be asked to make predictions about what they think will happen next. At each stopping point, students' predictions are recorded on the board or on an overhead-projector transparency. As the reading progresses, the accuracy of the predictions is tested.

In addition to the DL-TA, students take notes while they listen, and the notes are shared at the end of each session. During the first several sessions, the teacher melds the students' notes and asks one student to serve as a secretary. The secretary organizes the notes from the board and reproduces them in time for the next class. At the next class, students review the notes and check them for accuracy before the reading begins.

After the teacher has modeled the DL-TA and notetaking procedures for a few weeks, both activities are turned over to pairs of students. Usually, students choose their own partners, so there are two pairs of students responsible for sharing each chapter with the class. Each team does either the DL-TA or the notetaking activity with one of the latter six chapters of *The Twenty-One Balloons*. In a class of twenty-four students, each student can be involved in one of the activities. In larger classes, groups of three have worked together successfully. The advantages of working in pairs, however, are obvious. The students help each other through a careful reading of the text, and in the DL-TA they support each other in clarifying the inferential-type questions they ask the class.

The pairs doing the DL-TAs will need approximately three twenty-minute periods to read each of the six chapters to the class. The following instructions are given to these students, who are given a week to prepare their presentations:

1. Read the chapter together and find good stopping points. These are places where you can ask the class what they think will happen next.

2. Write questions for each stopping point.

3. Decide what parts each of you will read, and practice your reading.

4. Meet with me to discuss your work.

5. Make your presentation.

6. Meet with me for an evaluation.

Students are evaluated on how well-organized they were, the quality of their stopping points, their tact and politeness, and the degree of probing—that is, the degree to which they followed up on student predictions. (A similar procedure can be used to teach required basal stories. See Bear and Invernizzi 1984 for more details on organizing and evaluating student-directed reading groups.)

The instructions for the teams of notetakers are quite simple:

1. Read the chapter together and list the important points in an outline form.

2. Meet with me to share your notes.

3. Lead the class in a notetaking session following each day's reading.

4. Revise your notes to take into account additions suggested by the class.

5. Duplicate and distribute the notes before the next session.

6. Meet with me for an evaluation.

The teams are evaluated on the basis of the accuracy, clarity, and organization of their notes; their willingness to incorporate other students' suggestions; and their promptness in distributing the notes.

The First Round of Projects

As the reader may recall, the book begins with Professor Sherman's lecture to the Explorers' Club about his trip. He goes on at some length describing his craft and his preparation for the trip. In addition, some of the most famous balloonists create fantastic exhibitions in his honor. In the course of discussing the first four chapters, students often raise factual-type questions such as the following:

How wide is the United States?

How long does it take to travel across country by train?

How many miles per day can a balloon travel?

Who was president of the United States in 1883?

What is ballast?

How can salt water be turned into drinking water?

Where is Krakatoa?

Quite informally, the teacher asks students to find answers to these questions and to report back to the class the next day.

After these first few questions are answered, work groups are created to research broader topics. Usually there are three or four groups studying volcanoes and three groups studying balloon travel. Occasionally there is a group of students interested in inventions; these students read some of Du Bois's other works and study Rube Goldberg inventions. All of the groups work together, meet on a regular basis to do library research, write reports, and make group presentations. The teacher circulates among the groups and offers assistance as it is needed. Working together in groups is a new experience for many students, and we see this first round of projects as helpful in building a cooperative spirit in our class. Two to three weeks are allowed for preparation and presentations. Since students are required to develop bibliographies, the teacher presents separate lessons on how to do so.

Presentations are evaluated by the entire class. At first, the evaluations simply consist of students saying what they liked about a presentation. This remains the first step, but gradually, as a level of trust is developed, the presenters are asked to reflect on how they could have improved their presentation, and then their classmates make suggestions. Without fail, other groups pick up on these suggestions. Occasionally, since personal letter writing is also part of the sixth-grade curriculum, students have been asked to write letters to the groups that commented on their presentations.

The Second Round of Projects

The students' DL-TA presentations and notetaking presentations take the class to the point in *The Twenty-One Balloons* where the Gourmet Constitution is described. When students are asked what the next round of projects should be, without fail they suggest that

each student should choose a letter of the alphabet and then research that country. Students work in pairs and draw a letter out of
a hat. When the unit is team-taught, the alphabet is divided in half
and students choose a letter.

Our study of world geography is now under way. As a class, we
brainstorm on each letter and suggest possibilities for the pairs to
consider. Here some guidance is necessary. Unlike Du Bois, we do
not allow A to represent the United States. It is not unusual for students to confuse states with countries (last year a student suggested
Kansas for the letter C). Pairs settle on a country and place a flag on
their country on the world map. Typically, each pair is responsible
for creating a travel brochure for their country. Students contact
local travel agencies for brochures. (We've learned to call the agencies in advance of the assignment to warn them of the upcoming del-
uge. In some instances, as in the case of Lebanon, travel agencies are
unable to offer much assistance.) After a lesson on how to write a
business letter, students write their country's embassy in New York
for more information.

Finally, an international lunch is scheduled. Each pair brings a
dish, and parents are invited to join the classes in the cafeteria for an
international feast. Students wear native dress, and each pair is
given a moment in front of the group to introduce their country and
dish. This year, a local restaurant donated some extra food, paper
goods, and a tank of helium for a balloon launch. Students attached
letters to their balloons asking anyone who found the balloons to
write back and let us know where and when the balloons were retrieved. A strong southwesterly wind took several balloons twenty
miles to Connecticut in just forty-five minutes. In other years, the
balloons have gotten only as far as the local elementary school. On
the average, six out of forty balloons are retrieved.

Conclusion

Group work is an important part of this unit of study. At the beginning, groups were informal and established for short durations. In
previous grades, students may not have had opportunities to work
together, and it may require a few assignments before they take
their work seriously. Groups become productive when the students
see that they are in charge, that their peers will look to them for advice, and that they are responsible for leading the rest of the class.
We prefer to teach with a "little t," and not a "big t"; we prefer not
to tell our students what to do, but rather to facilitate their learning.

References

Bear, D. R., and M. Invernizzi. 1984. Student Directed Reading Groups. *Journal of Reading* 28 (December): 248–52.

Du Bois, W. P. 1947. *The Twenty-One Balloons.* New York: Viking.

Stauffer, R. G. 1975. *Directing the Reading-Thinking Process.* New York: Harper and Row.

23 Scriptwriting in Small Groups

Carole Cox
Louisiana State University

Overheard as three third-grade boys brainstormed ideas for a script for a videotape production:

> We can do anything we want with this video machine. Like Godzilla's fire. Like on that Dr. Pepper commercial and he was burning everything up and they gave him a Dr. Pepper. Fire all over the place. Maybe another planet. We need to make muscles and buildings and a little cable car that flies. And like this could be a time capsule. We need popsicle sticks. And a trap for Godzilla's feet. No trap! Godzilla's trying to save us from creatures from space. We need to make a background. You know how backgrounds move and they change things electronically? *And I could get my hamster to talk and Godzilla could save him! Yeah!*

Students like these, who create original scripts in small groups for a drama or media production about school subjects, events, literature, or just something they like (such as Godzilla), have a unique opportunity to use language and learn cooperatively. One approach to scriptwriting in small groups that I have found effective from primary through middle school begins with a general topic selected by the whole class. The topic is then discussed, debated, elaborated on, organized, explained, written about in separate parts in small groups, and finally put together for production by the whole class. The real payoff in cooperative learning is in the class's communication of their original ideas to an audience. These ideas have been revised and refined through small-group interaction, as the students literally acted on what they knew and brought their words and ideas in the script to life by performing or producing their own play or media production.

The Scriptwriting Process

1. *Selecting a topic.* Students are constantly in the process of generating topics that can be written about, dramatized, or produced in

media form. Examples include books that are read aloud to the whole class, social studies or science study, current events, popular films, other media events, and learning the use of a new medium. The suggestion to dramatize, film, or videotape these topics may come from the teacher after observing students spontaneously taking on characters, playing roles together, and creating their own improvised drama.

2. *Extending the response to the topic through talking and writing.* Younger children can dictate a group story that can be recorded as a language experience, or they can write their own stories or tell them to you. Older students may note ideas and extend these through personal writing.

3. *Sharing stories.* At some point, children may want to share what they have written with you, with the other members of a small group, or with the whole class. These sharings can become a focal point for discussing and extending ideas into scriptable form.

4. *Forming groups.* After sharing, students will have reasons to become connected in small groups and will suggest their own combinations. I have always found it more effective to let common interests, ideas, or images (such as Godzilla) override more traditional bases for forming groups such as ability or compatibility.

5. *Brainstorming ideas.* After grouping, allow a period for small-group discussions of the focal idea first, then periodic discussions with the whole class to point out a general direction for the script to follow.

6. *Blocking the script.* One way to organize ideas among the whole class is to classify them under the following types of headings on the board or on a large wall chart or overhead projector: Story Idea, Synopsis, Plot, Setting, Characters, Action, Events, Sequence.

7. *Recording results.* One student can record the group's ideas for each heading. The group can then put the ideas on a bulletin board for the whole class to use as a framework for future discussions and writing. Students can make notes and share ideas on this public draft.

8. *Dividing the sequence of events/actions into numbered acts.* A shift in groups may take place here according to their evolving interests and ability to work together cooperatively and productively. At this point *they* are in charge and will decide these things themselves if the script is developing well and still holding their interest.

9. *Writing acts in small groups and adding dialogue.* This stage will cover an extended period of time until each group has a working draft they can share. Many skills can be introduced or reinforced here, such as ordering and sequencing events and actions, writing dialogue, using quotation marks, writing narration, and noting stage directions or shooting notes.

10. *Coming together as a whole class to share written acts.* Discuss progress here, as well as transitions between acts. (This can be done periodically during the writing period.)

11. *Revise the acts in small groups.* The groups can begin to work with others to create transitions between acts; that is, from Act 1 to Act 2, Act 2 to Act 3, etc.

12. *Reviewing and revising the script as a group.* Copies of the working scripts should be available so that all can read and respond to them during periods of writing. All of the acts can be kept in a single folder so that students will have access to them as they get new ideas.

13. *Synthesizing the final script.* One working script will finally emerge, but changes will naturally occur as you begin to mount the play or media production. In the end, the script is a blueprint for the play or media production, not the production itself.

Integrating the Curriculum: *The Tale of an Unfair Election*

A play composed by a fourth- and fifth-grade combination class working in small groups was a natural outgrowth of a variety of interests that were organized, clarified, and communicated to others through dramatization. The subject is an example of how natural it is to integrate the curriculum through writing and drama.

I had read aloud a book written by my father, Gordon D. Shirreffs, who is primarily a writer of adult historical novels of the West, but who has also written many historical novels or novels with a Western setting for children and young adults (Cox 1986). The students were excited about *The Mystery of the Haunted Mine* and especially liked the three main characters, often speculating that the girl in the story was really me. I noticed that they were spontaneously playing at being Gary, Tuck, and Sue, and I also somewhat uncomfortably realized that Sue began to manifest mannerisms I knew were my own. These characters also began to appear in the students' writing, and it seemed only natural at this point to suggest scriptwriting in order to organize these improvisational character sketches into dramatic form. We began, then, with three main characters. But we needed a setting, a plot, and a lot of action.

The students were doing one Elementary Science Studies unit called "Where is the Moon Tonight?" and another unit called "Buds and Twigs." As a result, the play's setting became another planet peopled by two races: the Plant People and the Humanoids. The conflict in the play came from another topical interest—a social studies unit on elections during a presidential election year. The play began to take form when the students titled it *The Tale of an Unfair Election* and went through the steps of scriptwriting in small groups already described.

Here is the plot of *The Tale of an Unfair Election* written as promotional publicity for the play:

> An election takes place on the planet Zot. The election has been rigged by the Humanoid presidential candidate, Taylor. The Humanoids are invaders from a dying planet and have enslaved the native Plant People. Trailing Arbutus, the other presidential candidate, sends his vice-presidential candidate, Leaf, to earth for help to restore free elections for Plants and Humanoids alike.
>
> Leaf meets the Metzenberg children, Gary, Tuck, and Sue, who take him to their father, a famous space scientist who is going on a scientific expedition to Zot. He takes Leaf along and promises to help. The children stowaway on the spaceship U.S.S. Moonbeam and join their father for many adventures on Zot.

This play was performed in the round on the floor of the gym. The audience sat in a circle of chairs around the action. Spaces were left at intervals in the circle for entrances and exits, and the children waited behind screens outside the circle. To create an effect of deep space, the room was dark except for spotlights on the action. Audience involvement was invited during scenes with political rallies and revolt: the audience became part of the crowd and the drama itself.

The Individual and the Small Group: "Jan Andrews *is* Trailing Arbutus!"

While *The Tale of an Unfair Election* was considered a success for everyone, one student in particular appeared to benefit. Jan was the shyest child in the class and often struggled to look people in the eye when she spoke. She was also large for her age, a problem that compounded her shyness and her desire to remain unnoticed. I never asked Jan to speak or share, and she never volunteered.

Jan had become extremely involved with her small group, however, and when we cast the play with volunteers, Jan asked to play the important role of the presidential candidate of the Plant People, Trailing Arbutus. I think we were all surprised and not at all prepared for the transformation that took place when Jan donned the imperial-looking robes of the leader of the Plant People, a long and flowing hooded affair covered with plastic leaves attached with safety pins. She suddenly stood straighter, to the full advantage of her larger size. And as she gripped her robe and swished it about for emphasis, a voice emerged from inside the hood that none of us had ever heard before. It was similar to the voice of the quiet and very dignified young Jan, but it had a new edge of authority and volume. As they would say in the movies, "Jan Andrews *is* Trailing Arbutus!"

Jan outdid herself in this role and came to relish all drama-related experiences. The other children recognized her special talent and the transformation that took place when she worked on a script or put on a costume. For Jan, composing a play in the relative safety of a small group and then acting on it in the relative safety of a character constituted the special way that she found her own voice—one that was barely audible during whole-class activities but rang forth strong and clear when she created or played a role.

Other Dramatic Modes and Organizational Patterns for Small-Group Scriptwriting

In addition to scriptwriting for plays, there are several other ways students may practice cooperative learning in small groups and perhaps find the best mode of expression for their own voices. Filmmaking is almost always a collaborative effort of many individuals, and students who make films invariably work in small groups. Kindergartners can create draw-on films in which they work together to produce a segment of film that eventually becomes a part of a complete film for the whole class. First and second graders can use a Super 8 camera to plan and animate parts of a film produced by the whole class. By third and fourth grade, students can effectively work in small groups to produce short films of their own (Cox 1985). And by middle school, students can make individual films (although my experience has been that students prefer to work in small groups, especially those groups formed partly for social reasons). Even with individual filmmaking, however, the students will help each other during production of the films, with each serving as director/producer for his or her own film and as cameraperson/animator/technician/actor, etc. for the others' films (Cox 1984).

Video productions are less time-consuming than filmmaking since students may plan, script, film, and see the results of their work immediately. These productions are most effectively done in small groups since the medium lends itself to stringing many vignettes together in a television commercial, a news program, or a documentary. The portability of the equipment also facilitates this kind of production. The three third-grade boys described at the beginning of this paper eventually did produce a script featuring Godzilla as a main character. Their piece was combined with other vignettes to produce a TV commercial.

Other dramatic modes that lend themselves to students working cooperatively in small scriptwriting groups include readers theatre, puppetry, and the adaptation of literature to play production (Sloyer 1982).

What is most important in the end is not that a play or film or videotape is produced. It is that students like Jan Andrews find and use their own voices through scriptwriting and performing as they brainstorm, share, write, revise, and finally act on their own ideas in the fertile and relatively safe environment of a small group of other students who are also seeking to find and use their own voices.

References

Cox, C. D. 1984. Shooting for a Judy Award: A Documentary on Beginning Filmmakers. *English Journal* 73 (January): 46–50.

———1985. Filmmaking as a Composing Process. *Language Arts* 62: 60–69.

———1986. Gordon D. Shirreffs: An Interview with a Western Writer. *English Journal* 75 (April): 40–48.

Shirreffs, G. D. 1965. *The Mystery of the Haunted Mine.* New York: Scholastic Book Services.

Sloyer, S. 1982. *Readers Theatre: Story Dramatization in the Classroom.* Urbana, Ill.: National Council of Teachers of English.

Contributors

Corrine Alonso is coordinator of the Troy (Michigan) School District's Program for Accelerated and Creative Education for gifted and talented students. Prior to this position she spent eighteen years teaching French, Spanish, and English at Troy High School. Ms. Alonso also served as adjunct teacher from Syracuse University and taught the university's freshman English program at Troy High, allowing students to gain dual credit. In 1980 she was awarded a PAGE Scholarship from the English-Speaking Union, which allowed her to tour and study British schools. Ms. Alonso is currently enrolled in a Teaching the Talented program for graduate students at the University of Connecticut.

Donald R. Bear is an associate professor with the Center for Learning and Literacy in the College of Education, University of Nevada–Reno. His research has centered on the synchrony between stages of reading, writing, and spelling development. Specifically, he has examined the relationships between reading and writing fluency and orthographic awareness. Over the past year, Dr. Bear has concentrated on adult literacy proficiency and secondary reading. He directs a reading clinic for adults and is writing a manual for teachers integrating language-experience activities and oral history techniques in teaching adults.

E. Kathleen Booher teaches at Old Dominion University in Norfolk, Virginia. She has taught language arts and social studies in middle school, and English and composition in high school and college. She has also worked as a trainer for the New Jersey Writing Project at Rutgers University. In 1979, she won an *English Journal* Writing Award for her article, "Middle School Melancholia." In addition, she conducts summer writing project institutes and works as a K–12 consultant to school systems. She serves on the executive board of Peninsula Writers, an enthusiastic Michigan-based group of teacher-writers.

Jeffrey S. Copeland, a former high school language arts teacher, is currently an assistant professor of English education at the University of Northern Iowa. He is active in presenting workshops and inservice training sessions for language arts teachers. In addition to his journal articles, he has edited and designed four poetry texts: *Hiccups and Giggles, Creature Capers, Broccoli and Bubble Gum,* and *The Shooting Star: A Poetry Anthology.*

Carole Cox is an associate professor of curriculum and instruction at Louisiana State University, and has taught elementary school and directed drama programs for elementary and middle school students. In addition to journal articles and book chapters, she has recently published a college methods text, *Teaching Language Arts,* and is editing a book on film in the classroom for NCTE. She makes presentations regularly at NCTE conventions. Dr. Cox's current research interests are students' responses to literature and film.

Rex Easley is an assistant professor of English in the University College of the University of Cincinnati. In addition to teaching composition and creative writing courses, he is presently participating in a department-sponsored study of computer use in developmental writing courses. He has also published fiction in *Kansas Quarterly* and elsewhere.

Adele Fiderer is a helping teacher in English for Scarsdale Public Schools in New York. She works as a language arts consultant K–5 and also teaches writing and reading to a fifth-grade class. Her chapter in this book was developed through research in her own classroom. For the past four years she has coordinated a teacher-researcher program for her school district's teacher center. Ms. Fiderer has made presentations at conferences of NCTE, the New York State Department of Education, and the Metropolitan Schools Study Council of Teachers College, Columbia University. Currently a doctoral student in Teachers College, she is writing a dissertation on teacher-researchers.

Margaret Fleming is an associate professor of English and of language, reading, and culture at the University of Arizona. She is director of English education and codirector of the Southern Arizona Writing Project. She has taught high school English and written numerous articles for *English Journal, Arizona English Bulletin,* and other professional journals. For seven years Dr. Fleming also served as editor of *Arizona English Bulletin.* Two books, both coauthored with graduate-student colleagues, are *Teaching the Epic* and *Portraits: Biography and Autobiography in the Secondary School.*

Marie Foley is a lecturer in the Department of English at the University of California, Santa Barbara, where she teaches freshman composition and advanced composition. She has also taught English at the high school and community college levels. In addition to helping inaugurate and edit *Writers' Bloc,* a campus publication of winning student essays, she has written on advanced composition issues and on the five-paragraph essay. Dr. Foley is presently researching approaches to the teaching of form.

Carol Gilles is a doctoral student in reading at the University of Missouri. She has taught sixth grade, trained teachers to work with special needs students, and worked as a learning disabilities teacher for grades 7–9. She is currently president of the Mid-Missouri chapter of Teachers Applying Whole Language (TAWL). She makes presentations regularly at NCTE conventions and affiliate conferences.

Jeff Golub teaches English, speech communication, and precollege writing classes at Shorecrest High School in Seattle, Washington. He has taught at several other Washington high schools and junior high schools and was the chair of the English Department at Mattson Junior High School in Kent, Washington. Dr. Golub has spoken at several NCTE and Speech Communication Association conferences around the country and has conducted communications skills workshops for both school districts and businesses. His work with NCTE includes serving as coeditor of the "Junior High/Middle School 'Idea Factory'" column in *English Journal*, member of the Secondary Section Steering Committee and the Commission on the English Curriculum, and, currently, editor of the "Computers in the Classroom" column in *English Journal*. Dr. Golub is the editor of another Classroom Practices book, *Activities to Promote Critical Thinking*, and the author of many articles on speech communication and high school teaching.

Dana Herreman is a teacher of American literature, composition, and debate in the Newark City Schools in Newark, Ohio, where she has taught for twelve years. She has published a number of articles in state publications as well as in NCTE's *NOTES Plus*. Four years ago she participated in the Newark Excellence in Writing Project and studied the writing process with Dan Kirby at the University of Illinois. As a part of her school district's curriculum development committee, she directs a writing project for teachers. She is a member of three NCTE affiliates and served on the steering committee for the 1987 Ohio Council of Teachers of English/Language Arts conference, "Celebrating the Teacher."

John Kendall teaches English at the Upper School of Rutgers Preparatory School. He has served on the executive board of the New Jersey Council of Teachers of English; has edited their newsletter, *FOCUS*; and has cochaired a state writing conference at Lakewood, New Jersey. Mr. Kendall has taught writing workshops at local, state, and national English conferences. He has had two children's novels published, and has written two other novels for young adults.

Kirsten Barfod Levinsohn taught second grade for four years at Rutgers Preparatory School in Somerset, New Jersey. She received her master's degree in elementary/early childhood education at Rutgers University in New Brunswick, New Jersey, and her bachelor's degree at Williams College in Williamstown, Massachusetts. She is currently teaching preschool in Ann Arbor, Michigan.

Deborah Lohman has taught sixth grade for the last eight years in the Shoreham-Wading River Middle School in Shoreham, New York. Previously she was educational coordinator of Sleepy Hollow Restorations, Westchester, New York. Her interest in integrated curriculum and collaborative learning was piqued by a year working in the British Infant Schools. Ms. Lohman has recently completed a National Science Foundation Grant integrating science into all areas of the elementary curriculum.

Earl D. Lomax is an assistant professor of English at David Lipscomb College in Nashville, Tennessee, where he also directs the program in English education. He taught at the junior high and high school levels before pursuing the Ph.D. in English education at the University of Missouri. He is active in both the Nashville and Tennessee Council of Teachers of English and is a frequent book reviewer for *The ALAN Review*. Dr. Lomax has been a program participant at annual meetings of the Conference on English Education and NCTE. He was awarded a faculty research grant for the summer of 1988 to work on a book dealing with young adult literature.

Virginia McCormick teaches English at William Allen High School, Allentown, Pennsylvania. She has taught grades K–12. Ms. McCormick is the author of a teacher's manual for a secondary writing text and has served as an editor and consultant for numerous educational publishers. A frequent contributor to NCTE publications, Ms. McCormick has also had articles published in *Education Week* and *The New England Journal of Medicine*. She makes presentations regularly at NCTE conventions. Ms. McCormick was named one of the outstanding secondary educators in America in 1975 and received the Pennsylvania Innovative Teaching Award in 1984.

G. Douglas Meyers is an associate professor in the Department of English at the University of Texas at El Paso. He has published numerous articles on writing and writing pedagogy, including the areas of expository, technical, and business writing. Dr. Meyers directs the West Texas Writing Project, and in 1986 was awarded the Outstanding University English Teacher award by the local NCTE affiliate, the Paso del Norte Council of Teachers of English.

Tom Morton teaches English at Prince of Wales Secondary School in Vancouver, British Columbia, and trains teachers in cooperative learning throughout the province. Some of his work appears in *Structuring Cooperative Learning: The 1987 Handbook*, by David and Roger Johnson, and in William Glasser's *Control Theory in the Classroom*. He also wrote *Look Again: The Process of Prejudice and Discrimination* and *Hard Times Then and Now*.

Muriel Ridland is a lecturer in the composition program of the English Department at the University of California, Santa Barbara. She has taught composition and literature there and at California State University, Los Angeles. Her degrees were taken at the University of New Zealand, Canterbury College. She collaborated with John Ridland in writing *And Say What He Is: The Life of a Special Child*. Dr. Ridland recently lectured to students training to become teachers of English at Eötvös Loránd University in Budapest, discussing current composition teaching in the United States.

Barbara Schoen is an associate professor of language arts at the State University of New York, College at Purchase, and is director of the college's writing program. In addition to her work at SUNY, Dr. Schoen has published two novels, as well as short stories and articles both popular and academic.

Caryl Klein Sills is an assistant professor of English and director of writing at Monmouth College in West Long Branch, New Jersey. She has presented papers on writing theory at conferences sponsored by NCTE and the New Jersey College English Association, and she has developed writing across the curriculum workshops for several New Jersey colleges. Dr. Sills is a founding member of New Jersey Computer Users in Education and has recently published articles on the effects of computer-assisted writing instruction on freshman writers. Currently, she is studying paired sections of a freshman composition course to compare and evaluate traditional and computer-assisted methods of writing instruction.

Mary K. Simpson-Esper teaches seventh-grade language arts. She has had seventeen years of classroom experience teaching for the Prince William County Public Schools in Woodbridge, Virginia. In 1985, she became a teacher/consultant with the Northern Virginia Writing Project at George Mason University. She has had articles published in several professional journals, including *Virginia Journal of Education, Journal of Reading,* and *Language Arts.*

S. Phyllis M. Taufen, SNJM, is an assistant professor of English at Gonzaga University, Spokane, Washington, where she teaches English composition and business communication for the School of Business. She has directed the University Writing Lab and is coordinator of Lower Division English. Nominated for Teacher-of-the-Year in 1985, she is widely known in the Northwest for her workshops for educators and business leaders. She is actively involved in the Washington State Council of Teachers of English, the Inland Northwest Council of Teachers of English, and the National Writing Project.

Edgar H. (Herb) Thompson is an assistant professor of education and director of elementary education at Emory & Henry College, Emory, Virginia. He has published articles in several journals, including *English Journal, English Education,* and *NOTES Plus.*

Sharon E. Tsujimoto most recently taught at a Montessori elementary school, grades 1–3. She has also taught grades K–12 at private and public schools in Hawaii. Ms. Tsujimoto worked as a part-time teacher for a Chapter I reading program for a number of years and also taught first grade at a private school in New York City.

Marc VanDover is a secondary learning disabilities teacher at Jefferson Junior High in Columbia, Missouri. He has taught elementary-age students with behavior problems in a self-contained setting. Mr. VanDover has made presentations at meetings of Teachers Applying Whole Language and the Missouri IRA, and at local district inservice programs.

Richard Whitworth is a professor of English at Ball State University, where he teaches methods in English courses. In 1987, Lambda Iota Tau selected him as one of four outstanding professors of English; also in 1987, he received the Steinbeck Research Institute's Outstanding English

Teacher award. During his career, Dr. Whitworth taught language arts at all levels—elementary, junior high/middle school, and high school. His articles have appeared in *English Journal, Clearing House, Learning,* and *Journal of Secondary Education.* He is currently investigating the potential of laser disc instruction in the teaching of English.

DATE DUE

DEC 1 4 2004			
GAYLORD			PRINTED IN U.S.A.